Advance Praise for
Get-It-Done Guy's 9 Steps to Work Less and Do More

"If you're serious about becoming successful, you not only need clarity around your long-term purpose, vision, and goals, you need to organize your time, space, and attention to make success possible. This book will show you how to make sure all your efforts count, so every moment you choose to work brings you closer to your dreams. Stever's unique style makes this book both highly practical and a fun, engaging read."

—**Jack Canfield**, coauthor of
The Success Principles and Chicken Soup for the Soul® series

"Whether you're a C-suite executive or just starting your career, you need to be able to produce results fast. Stever gives simple, practical advice for eliminating distractions, honing in on what's most important, and reaching your goals faster and with more fun. Put his advice into action and increase your impact!"

—**Keith Ferrazzi**, *New York Times* #1 bestselling author of *Who's Got Your Back* and *Never Eat Alone*

"Building your mojo in work and life means doing what makes you happy and gives you meaning. This book's nuts-and-bolts advice will help you concentrate your efforts on what matters most to you and to find ways to achieve it simply and quickly."

—**Marshall Goldsmith**, *New York Times* and
Wall Street Journal #1 bestselling author of
What Got You Here Won't Get You There and *MOJO: How to Get It,
How to Keep It, and How to Get It Back When You Lose It!*

"Stever Robbins has taken a practical, useful topic—how to get more done—and applied it to getting more done at work, and more done in building a meaningful life. The book is packed with tips you can use immediately, and its humor, style, and irreverence make it an easy, fun read."

—**Marci Shimoff**, *New York Times* bestselling author of *Happy for No Reason* and *Chicken Soup for the Woman's Soul*

"For years, Stever Robbins has been giving me advice. His podcast and now his book are an important source of advice for me. What are you waiting for? You have to pick this up."

—**Chris Brogan**, *New York Times* bestselling author of *Trust Agents* and *Social Media 101*

"Wisdom plus tools to make you a heck of a lot more productive! A big payoff for a small book!"

—**Leonard Schlesinger**, president, Babson College; former vice chairman and COO, Limited Brands

"Some paths to a better life involve twelve steps. Robbins saves you three. His nine steps help me, and I know they will help you live better and get more done by working more efficiently and effectively. Even if you love your work, his advice helps!"

—**Howard Stevenson**, chairman, National Public Radio; Sarofim-Rock Baker Foundation Professor, Harvard Business School

"The Get-it-Done Guy provides a wealth of smart, useful ways to save time, conveyed with a delightful sense of humor and fun. This book isn't just about doing things better and faster; it's about how to build an aligned life and career, focused on your highest goals and values."

—**Frances Hesselbein**, Distinguished Chair of Leadership, U.S. Military Academy; former CEO, Girl Scouts of America; awarded U.S. Presidential Medal of Freedom

Get-It-Done Guy's

9 Steps to Work Less and Do More

STEVER ROBBINS

ST. MARTIN'S GRIFFIN ❧ NEW YORK

GET-IT-DONE GUY'S 9 STEPS TO WORK LESS AND DO MORE. Copyright © 2010 by Stever Robbins. All rights reserved. Printed in the United States of America. For information, address St. Martin's Press, 175 Fifth Avenue, New York, N.Y. 10010.

www.stmartins.com

Book design by Kelly S. Too

ISBN 978-0-312-66261-5

First Edition: September 2010

10 9 8 7 6 5 4 3 2 1

To people who have made a big difference in my life,
knowingly or not, and what they taught me:

Q—There's always a better way;

Len Schlesinger—Fundamentally, there are just three things
you need to know;

Michael Neill—Settle for nothing less than passion, it will find
you;

Richard Bandler—It's all in your mind;

Apurva Patel—You are who you decide you are;

Jamie Kent—You can be laid back and still change the world;

Tamin Pechet—Dream big then take a first step;

Matt Doyle—The job is auditioning, performing is the bonus.

CONTENTS

GET-IT-DONE GUY'S
9 STEPS TO WORK LESS AND DO MORE

INTRODUCTION

Once upon a time, they promised us paradise. We invented machines and discovered electricity. We could make clothes, build houses, and do stuff better than we ever could before. Where this was leading was obvious: a world where we spend all our time living for our passion. We become artists and philosophers, dress in flowing, comfortable clothes, and use our matter duplicators to provide for our daily needs. Right.

It didn't work out that way. Instead, those of us who are employed work longer hours than ever. We all work *way* harder than our hunter-gatherer ancestors ever worked. Our lifespan is about three times what theirs was, too. That's the good news. The bad news is that we spend so much of that working, we probably end up with less actual fun during our lifetime.

I've never liked hard work. At age twelve, I discovered computers. What wonderful devices! Figure out a solution to a problem, program it in, and the computer will solve it for you again and again. It was a lazy middle-schooler's dream; I had discovered my first tool to work less. I could solve problems once, and spend all that free time eating Cheetos and playing Pong (if you're under thirty-five, think of Pong as Halo III with a one-pixel screen). While I was blissfully munching Cheetos, the business world also discovered how to work less with computers, Day-Timers, and calculators. As they happily prioritized tasks, they never talked about working less and doing more. Instead, they used the impressive-sounding word *productivity*. Suddenly, it was all the buzz. By the late eighties, productivity had become entrenched as our national religion. Want to win an argument? Just say, "My idea will make us more productive." The Holy Grail of productivity is so deeply ingrained that your opponents will lay down their swords, bow their heads, and defer. After all, what could be better than an idea that will make us more productive? No one even bothers to ask. And that's a real shame. Because if you look closely, you'll notice that being more productive isn't doing much for us individually.

Part of the problem is structural: The benefits of productivity don't get spread evenly. So if you want to get stuff done faster and actually have it improve your life by allowing you to work less, you have to do things that will help you work less and do more in *all* areas of your life.

That's where I come in. A career in startups and ten years coaching entrepreneurs, businesspeople, and students has given me ample opportunity to help people in all walks of life get their chaos under control so they can start working less, doing more, and having the life of their dreams—even if that just means eight hours of sleep each night! On top of this, I'm an organization geek myself. On a bright, sunny afternoon, my idea of a good time is visiting a stationery store to buy new pens and then organizing all my pens based on which ink flows best on the beautiful sixty-pound satin-finish notebook paper I also just bought. Yes, I'm pasty white. And what might once have been a therapy-inducing obsession has given me the ability to help people with tans get organized. Life works in mysterious ways.

Unless you're reading this book for the sheer joy of reading—in which case, you have odd taste in leisure reading—you bought this book believing life will be better by owning it. Maybe you want to overcome your procrastination habit, untether yourself from your technology, or learn how to beat distractions and focus better. Those are good goals. Maybe you've heard my Get-It-Done Guy podcast and want to support me because you love me, you *really* love me. That's an even better goal.

Fortunately for those of you who want a better life full of working less and doing more, most of *my* life has been spent in a neurotically compulsive drive to figure out how to do everything better, stronger, and faster. There are dozens of ways to streamline everything you do, from managing multiple projects at once, to dealing with tidal waves of incoming cruft that pervades the modern work world, to even caring for your macaroni and glitter sculpture of Queen Elizabeth.

I've reduced the quest to work less and do more down to 9 simple steps. Each step will help you work less. A lot of what we humans do doesn't serve us very well. It doesn't move us toward our goals, it doesn't make us happy, and it makes us chip our nails and need manicures.* It's time to change that. Each step will also help you do more. Once you've stopped with the work that isn't serving you, you'll learn to do what you're already doing, but in different ways. You'll learn to recognize when you can get a little more oomph out of life without putting in any more oomph. In fact, you might be able to put in some "aaaahhhhh . . . yum" and get a little more oomph. And if that isn't everyone's dream, I don't know what is! With these 9 steps you'll be working less and doing more in no time:

---

* It's the twenty-first century, men. Manicures are very hip.

STEP 1: LIVE ON PURPOSE. If you're anything like me, a lot of what you call work has very little to do with getting anything important done in life. Like when I compulsively check my social media sites every hour. That kind of thing must go.

STEP 2: STOP PROCRASTINATING. What is procrastinating except the very art of not doing the very stuff you know is most important? We'll cover how to nip this in the bud, or at least arrange for someone to kick you into action when you're delaying. And just in case you're someone who claims being kicked into action doesn't work for you, we'll get out an ostrich feather and tickle you into action instead.

STEP 3: CONQUER TECHNOLOGY. Our supposed savior, technology, is for many of us the greatest obstacle we have to being truly productive. You'll learn how to use your technology to help you focus, instead of . . . hey, hang on a second. There's an instant message coming in. . . .

STEP 4: BEAT DISTRACTIONS TO CULTIVATE FOCUS. Do you have any idea how much time is wasted multitasking? A lot. If you eliminate distractions and keep yourself focused, you can toss yourself into the kind of flow where the results come fast and easy. And you'll do it entirely without the use of pharmaceutical supplements.

STEP 5: STAY ORGANIZED. When you have a place for everything and everything is in its place, it's no work at all to find what you need, when you need it. I'm not just talking about physical clutter; this is also about organizing your thinking, your projects, and your processes. Reclaim all that time you otherwise spend hunting for the next step, the next paper, or the next person by knowing exactly where to go and what to do when you need it.

STEP 6:   STOP WASTING TIME.   Sometimes you appear to be doing exactly, precisely what you should be doing but are actually wasting time that could be spent doing something more meaningful, like eating bonbons and sipping fruit-flavored beverages in a hammock strung between your computer and your door frame.

STEP 7:   OPTIMIZE.   Doing things twice bores me silly. *Especially* when it comes to making mistakes. In this step you'll learn how to do things once or twice, streamline them to the point where the task is completely brainless, and . . . Let's just say that I'll leave you to connect the dots. Think, "brain-eating Zombies." The implications will jump right out.

STEP 8:   BUILD STRONGER RELATIONSHIPS.   You can't get there alone; you need someone to program the GPS while you're trying to read street signs. Relationships are, ultimately, how everything gets done. Together, we can do far, far more than we can alone. For example, one of us can measure while the other mixes, and then we can both eat the cookies when they're ready. You'll learn some excellent ways to create and deepen the relationships that matter most.

STEP 9:   LEVERAGE.   The ultimate in doing more, our final destination of leverage will give you several ways to make sure when you do get results, you get better, stronger, and faster than you'd ever dreamed possible.

With each step, you'll reclaim more and more of your life. You will begin to see the light at the end of the tunnel. Your shoulders will feel lighter and your body will vibrate with energy as you wander through fields of lilies. That's because with each step, you'll find yourself honing in on the things that actually move you forward, and learning the skills you need to resist the busy-ness that pulls you away from what you're trying to achieve.

These steps aren't just theory! They have come from years of working with clients, helping them make actual changes in their lives. Each one will come with stories, examples, and specific tips that show you how the step can be applied in many different areas throughout your life. With these 9 steps you'll do so much more, and you'll work so much less, that your boss will promote you; your husband, wife, spousal equivalent, or polyamorous family unit will beam proudly; and your kids will gasp in awe and blame you for everything just a little bit less than they currently do.

A WORK LESS, DO MORE WARNING

A word of caution, however. Getting everything done in less time is wonderful, it's very wonderful. But it comes with a hidden dark side. If you aren't careful, you'll end up working *more* than when you started. That's why you absolutely must understand how to ensure this doesn't happen.

There's a lot more to life than getting stuff done, but if you aren't careful, you'll never find out. When you start to work less and do more, you'll be more productive. That's a good thing, right? Not necessarily! They promise if we get more productive, the economy will soar, and we'll be living the Good Life in a magical land of plenty. "They" are our secret, shadowy overlords. We follow their brainwashing and sometimes, we *do* get more productive. And the economy soars. That's all for the better, isn't it? Well, er, no. Not unless you happen to be the economy. And you aren't the economy, you're you.

From the perspective of you, it doesn't work that way. Haven't you noticed when you get more productive, your workload decreases but within a few months, you're back to your previous level of frantic? Or maybe even worse?

You start getting more done in less time, so you have more free time to enjoy the finer things in life, like eight hours' sleep. *But that free time doesn't stick around.*

Your boss swoops by, sees that you are taking time to inhale and exhale, and instantly gives you another project to work on . . . or, worse, *you* start to freak out after your third deep breath and frantically go looking for new work. Over time, every life improvement increases how many commitments you have. Your systems can handle a dozen projects at once, but *you* have limits. Our technology has sped up the world so now we don't wait for the world anymore, the world waits for us. *We* are the limiting factor. (All the more reason for the machines to revolt and do away with us.)

This book will be useful only if you get to enjoy the fruits of your own efforts. If you get better at what you do and then overload yourself, you're no better off. Pay close attention to the chapter on focus. After you've started saving time, say no when anyone asks you to take on new commitments—even if the anyone is you.

If necessary, don't tell anyone you're saving time. Continue to complain occasionally about your heavy workload and how you never seem to have as much free time as you want. Then spend your newfound free time doing things that are fun, meaningful, and life-enriching!

Along with this book, you'll find a resource Web site at GetIt DoneGuyBook.com that will include links to tools, information, books, and other resources to help you put these principles to work. Once we're all working less and doing more, we'll take all that time and effort we're saving and have one heck of a party. It will feature fruit-flavored beverages, Oreo ice cream cake, and celery stuffed with hummus for those who prefer a low-carb diet.

I hope you enjoy taking this journey as much as I enjoyed creating it. Now go on; your free time is waiting.

STEP 1

LIVE ON PURPOSE

Here's the number one principle and our first step to working less in your life: Stop doing stuff that doesn't help you reach your goals. It sounds simple, doesn't it? It's a shame almost no one does it. The most common way we work more and do less is by working on the wrong stuff. We spend our time doing, doing, doing, even if the doing has nothing to do with our goals, business, or life. Surely I'm not the only one who has spent five hours a day spewing one-line nonsense "status updates" on my favorite social media Web site, and then wondered why I'm running so hard just to stay in the same place.

Of course, it's much easier to say "work on what's important" than it is to do it. In this first step to working less and doing more we will explore how lacking clarity about our goals both at work and at home can be our doom. I will help you overcome this problem so that you never waste time working on the wrong stuff ever again—or at least not when you follow my advice. In this chapter you will learn how to identify your ultimate goals for every situation. Then I'll explain how you can develop a life map so you'll know when you're on track and when you're just fooling yourself with busywork.

You can get hijacked into nonsense-land when you don't know what you want. Before you can streamline life, you must know your goals. If you don't know where you're going, you can't make getting there effortless. When you know your destination, you can chart a course in advance. Moment-by-moment, you can make sure you're doing things that take you where you want to go. Otherwise, all your activity is nothing more than busyness.

We'll start by making sure we're doing the *right* things. It's not always obvious, though sometimes your gut tells you there's got to be a better way. My friend Michael discovered that as a parent.

MEET MICHAEL

Michael was mortified. His teenager Skyler's room was, to put it mildly, like an antechamber from the inner circle of heck: strange growths on the walls, mysterious smells belching forth from unidentifiable piles beneath the bed. At night, shrieking cries could be heard from behind the closed bedroom door (is that what kids today call music?). Michael's solution was simple: Ask Skyler to clean up. When that didn't work, he offered video games as bribes. And when *that* didn't work, he resorted to yelling. Soon, Michael was nearing a nervous breakdown. Skyler, however, just turned up the stereo one notch and went back to whatever it is that teenagers do inside their lairs.

As Michael told this story, I tried to imagine his life. My time is spent dancing through life, smelling daffodils and singing songs. Michael's time is spent obsessing about his teenager's room. He plots and plans and bribes. When we have lunch, he hardly notices my unbelievably witty and insightful conversation. Instead, he moans about his son the whole time. As if living with the youngster wasn't bad enough, he must relive every agonizing moment out loud. Michael realized something wasn't working about the situation, but he had no idea what to do. He was providing a living case study of the most important thing you'll ever learn: The key to working less is being on purpose.

Michael doesn't wake up thinking, "My life purpose is having a kid with a clean bedroom." At some point, he decided a clean bedroom was important. He thought it was the path to some *other* goal. Sadly, he's forgotten the other goal and is fixated on the whole room thing. This happens to all of us—we get distracted and lose sight of our ultimate goals. We decide we want to finish that project at work by tomorrow, so we e-mail our coworker Bernice to get her notes on the project. Her response is so engaging that six hours later, we suddenly realize we've had a fabulous bonding experience with Bernice and done no work on the report.

YOU NEED TO IDENTIFY YOUR GOALS

The first step in living on purpose is to get really good at identifying goals. Big goals, little goals, medium-sized goals. Everything you do at any moment has a bunch of goals attached. You see, goals don't hang out alone; they travel in packs. Really big goals—like "be successful"—are made up of subgoals. Those are made up of smaller subgoals, and so on. Finally at the bottom are specific, concrete actions. But all these subgoals offer enticing diversions where we can conveniently get off course, giving us the chance to waste time and energy. If a subgoal wanders off course, so do we, and we never get what we want. If your highest-level work goal was to be successful at work, the following table will show you how your goals might break down.

Highest level goal	**Be successful at work**
A subgoal of "Be successful at work"	Get promoted to Grand Poobah
A subgoal of "Get promoted"	Totally master current job
Specific action you take to reach the goal "Master current job"	Attend weekly status meeting

Yes, you can see that your subgoals of getting promoted and mastering your current job, and yes, even your action of attending weekly status meetings all relate to your highest-level work goal—being successful.

Michael's love of clean teenage bedrooms isn't one of his highest-level goals, it's a subgoal of some larger goal. My guess: Michael's high-level goal is to be a good parent. He believes he has to do that by teaching his son to be a responsible adult (which is a subgoal). And *his* parents brainwashed him into thinking that being a responsible adult means having a clean bedroom, which led to his action of yelling at Skyler to clean the bedroom.

Someone else with the same high-level goal of being a good parent might have different subgoals and use different actions as a result. Their subgoal might be to spend quality time with their kid and their action might be talking to their kid about school at dinner. Or perhaps they would play baseball together, or go out for manicures together, or play baseball *and* go out for manicures together. Heck, if it were me, I think teaching your kid to be a responsible adult means letting a kid keep their room however they want it, and letting *them* deal with the consequences when the pizza grows legs. Whatever your subgoals and actions, they'd better match your big goal. Otherwise while trying to be a good parent, you risk pulling a Michael. You'll spend your quality together-time yelling at your child and making them hate you.

This mismatch between goals and actions is hardly limited to parenting. One company I worked with had an overall goal of making it easy for an entire industry to adopt a new technology. A subgoal was raising funds from the board of directors, which included some prominent financiers. Their fund-raising subgoal's action was developing a prototype product to show the board. The investors would be so dazzled that they would write a big fat check. The prototype took on a life of its own, however. Even after money was raised, it lived on as an entirely separate project. It kept sucking up time and resources without contributing one bit to the original goal of building a product customers would buy. Here's how their goals broke down:

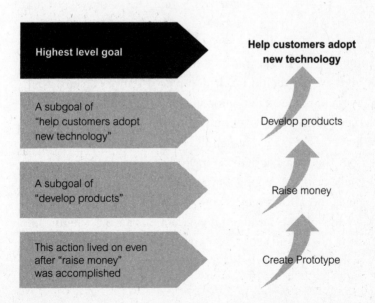

Highest level goal — Help customers adopt new technology

A subgoal of "help customers adopt new technology" — Develop products

A subgoal of "develop products" — Raise money

This action lived on even after "raise money" was accomplished — Create Prototype

MAKE SURE YOUR ACTIONS MATCH YOUR GOALS

Living on purpose means stopping to make sure your actions still match your big goals. But you need to keep the big picture in mind to do this. Without knowing your higher-level goals, you don't know whether your actions are helping.

To understand why the big picture is important, let's consider the time-honored, time-wasting tradition, the status meeting. You might think its purpose is obvious: Share status. Yes, but what's the goal of sharing status? What's the higher-level goal here? Is it to coordinate when one person's work depends on another's? Is it to build team cohesion? Is it to brainstorm solutions to project emergencies? Is it to have an excuse to eat fat-free, low-cal, diet donuts and decaf coffee? Without knowing the goals above "share status," it's hard to know if the meetings are even useful. If we're sharing status to coordinate—a higher-level goal—but people are already coordinating via e-mail, then the meeting is useless. Knowing the higher-level goals helps make sure our actions are still moving us forward.

If you know your higher goals off the top of your head, great! Knowing that will clue you in about what your lower-level subgoals and actions should be. It doesn't work in reverse, though. Knowing a lower-level action or subgoal gives you no clue about the larger goals. At least not until you ask "Why?"

When you get buried in details is when you risk wasting time on actions that won't actually help you reach your subgoals, high-level goals, or both. Asking why you are doing something serves as a check and always moves your focus back to the big picture. Asking why helps you find out if your actions have come unglued from your goals. In theory, you could do this as often as every day, reviewing your to-do list to make sure it ties to your bigger goals. In my perfect fantasy world, I check my actions against my goals every day. In real life, once a week or once every other week is more realistic.

Use a Goal Ladder to Check Your Actions and Goals

You can build a goal ladder around your actions to check them. A goal ladder is a quick, written recognition of how your actions and subgoals link to your larger goals. It lists your actions, the goals the action is trying to reach, the goals of that goal, and so on.

Poor Michael is yelling at his kid. That tells us nothing about his goals. Maybe he's worried the room is a health hazard. Or he has extradimensional sensitivity to messy rooms within a one-hundred-yard radius. Or maybe he's seeking unconscious revenge for the years he spent as a father when he really wanted to be pursuing an Olympic gold medal in squeegee juggling. We can build Michael's goal ladder by asking "Why?" to find his subgoals and highest-level goals.

"Why are you so concerned about Skyler's room?" I ask. "Because," Michael replies, "Skyler needs to learn to be responsible. That's my job as a parent, after all."

Aha! Michael just confirmed our earlier theory that he's really trying to be a good parent. Here's his whole goal ladder around yelling at Skyler:

PARENTING	
Main goal	Be a good parent.
Subgoal	Teach kids to be responsible adults.
Action	Demand kid clean room.

Now that it's starkly on paper, Michael can make sure his actions are meeting his ultimate goal of being a good parent. He does this by starting at his topmost goal and asking "How can I reach this goal?" If his answer isn't the same as his actions, he's found a mismatch. Here's what we found when I stepped him through the questions.

"Michael, how can you be a good parent?" I ask. "By helping Skyler become a responsible adult," he replies. So far, so good. His subgoal matches, so we know there's alignment, at least in Michael's mind. Let's go one more level.

"And how can you help Skyler become a responsible adult?"

"By letting Skyler make his own decisions and accept responsibility for the consequences."

Isn't *that* interesting? Michael *didn't* say, "By demanding Skyler clean his room." He wants Skyler to make decisions and accept the consequences. That's exactly what's happening! Skyler *is* deciding to have a messy room. He's handling the consequences, a yelling father, by turning the volume on his stereo up to eleven. But because he forgot his larger goals, Michael didn't notice he was achieving them.

Letting go of his room-cleaning fetish and redesigning his goal ladder so that it reflects his actual subgoals would serve Michael well. If he ignores his true subgoals and clings to the wrong actions, it will lead to nothing but trouble. He'll spend years in conflict. Skyler will move out and become independent, and instead of reigniting his Olympic ambitions, Michael will blow his savings on therapy to deal with having such an ungrateful offspring. Skyler will keep a neat apartment once there's no parent to rebel against, and life will go on. Michael's problem is that his goal ladder wasn't aligned.

When you feel dissatisfied, or when you're working too hard, the problem could be a mismatch between your goals and actions. Write out your goal ladder and make sure it all lines up. First start with your actions and ask "Why?" to find your subgoals. Keep asking why until you map up to your larger-level goals, at least two or three levels.

Now double-check the alignment by starting at the top. Ask "How can I reach this?" but don't peek at your existing subgoals or actions, just answer. *Then* look at your subgoals. If your answer doesn't match, you know your subgoals have become unhinged from your real goal. Then also look at your actions. If your actions don't ultimately jibe with your highest-level goals, your actions aren't working, either. Now either change your top-level goal or begin changing your subgoals and actions until they're in alignment.

Before getting better at what you're doing—which we'll get to later—you must make sure what you're doing matches all your goals and subgoals! Otherwise you'll just get better at doing the wrong thing. Getting better at doing the *right* thing is the key to working less and doing more. So let's discuss how to identify the goals at the top, which drive your entire goal ladder.

HOW TO IDENTIFY YOUR TOP GOALS

You may know what your own personal top-level goal is, but at work, the top goals come from the organization. It's usually called a vision or mission. The subgoals are strategic initiatives, and below that are projects or goals. Different companies have different names for them. All that's important is that they point you in the direction of meeting the topmost goals. If you were working for a financial software company, your goals might break down like this:

	BUSINESS	**ORGANIZATION LEVEL**
How?		
Vision	Become the world's foremost supplier of financial software.	Executives, VPs
Strategic initiative	Develop software to help people manage their checkbooks.	Directors
Project	Create Mac version of software.	Project managers
Actions	Write 1,000 lines of code.	Programmers
		Why?

If your actions don't match your projects, or your project doesn't fit the strategy, you can work your butt off and it won't help the company one bit. In fact, when earnings dip next, executives will scramble to "return to their core business." They will notice your project isn't adding value and lay you off, with genuine tears of dismay. At bonus time, they'll tearfully collect a bonus of 190 percent of their already-inflated base salary for having the strength to oversee such unpleasant and regretful layoffs. It will never cross their mind that it was their job to keep the organization aligned in the first place.*

If you're in a management position you can align your organization using the same tools we just used with Michael. Ask the people who actually do the work, "Why are you doing this?" Then ask their managers, and their managers, and their managers. You will end up with a neat map of what everyone *thinks* they should be doing.

---

* Yes, some companies have no mission, or they have a stated mission that is the opposite of how they act. Fixing *that* is going to take more than I can fit in a footnote, so for now, pretend your company has a mission.

Then do a sanity check. Make sure that if you ask "How?" to the biggest goals, the answer is at least vaguely related to the organization's subgoals. In most places, you'll find a mismatch—or several—somewhere along the way. A top goal may be "to provide excellent medical care for patients," and one of the intermediary goals may be "cut costs by 15 percent," which is being carried out by skimping on care quality, an action that clearly doesn't fit in with the top goal. If you find the conflict, but can't make it right yourself, your best bet is probably to work toward both the top and intermediary goals, knowing they can come into conflict. When you must choose between them, the choice is yours. The idealist in me says to do what's right for the patients. My realist says to do what's right for the patient, within the cost-cutting constraints. My cynic says to hunker down and cut costs, since the chances of anyone you know personally being killed by your inferior medical care are small enough that you can afford to ignore the moral implications of your actions and retreat into the justification that you would lose your job if you disregarded cost-cutting. And your job, presumably, is more important than someone else's life.

Remember our employees who created a prototype that became a completely separate development effort for their board of directors? If they had stopped to identify their goal in hour ten of the prototype, they would have realized that there were better uses of their time. For example, building a real product that would help their customers adopt the new technology in their industry.

CREATE A LIFE MAP SO YOU CAN LIVE ON PURPOSE!

If you're going to have a life of working less and doing more, I'm not going to let you do it just to feed the ever-gaping maws of your corporate overlords. The "do more" is all about doing *life*.

Specifically, *your* life. If you're a corporate overlord reading this, pretend for a moment that you're actually a normal human being who wants to live your own full, satisfying life. That's what we're all about.

Next we're going to create a Life Map you can use *every day* to know what is and isn't moving you in the direction you want. It will help you not only work less and do more of your ideal life, but find that work stops being work when you're living an aligned life. It becomes play.

A Life Map is simply a general goal ladder for your life. Rather than doing a separate goal ladder for every action you take, a Life Map lays out an overview of the different levels of goals in all aspects of your life.

Your Life Map starts with whatever a full, satisfying life is *for you*. It is the destination at the very top of your personal ladder of goals.

Write down your vision for your life. What do you hope to accomplish in this lifetime? This is for *you* to answer. Not your spouse, not your parents (*especially* not your parents), not the media, not your religious organization or your secular book club. What's *your* vision for your life?

A lifetime of taking your cues from everyone else can persuade you to want what they want, instead of what *you* want. A coaching client once landed the perfect job: a fabulous offer from a consulting firm that was a perfect match for, well, what everyone with his pedigree wanted. He didn't seem very excited when he told me. I pointed this out. He grinned sheepishly and admitted he wasn't really very interested in the job.

"Then why are you considering consulting?" I asked, incredulously. "Because that's what my parents would want," he replied. "Do you often make your choices based on what your parents want, rather than what you want?" I just had to know. "Yes," he said. Well, I just *had* to deliver the kindly felt, but still gleefully satisfying coup de grâce. "Does that work? Is it giving you the life you want?" He looked up in surprise. "No. I want to be a high school teacher."

It was a career his parents would not have chosen for him. It was a career his peers would not have chosen for him. But it is what he wanted. He hadn't admitted it to himself in years. When we spoke three months ago, he had just finished a semester as a teacher and loved it. Time will tell if it's the right full-time career for him. Either way, he's starting to leave behind everyone else's agenda for him and connect to his own.

Identify Your Life Vision

Ask yourself, "What would be a fulfilling life?" Be inspiring! Think about your role in the larger world. For example, "To raise my kids to have opportunity, happiness, and success." Or "To end poverty." Or "To be the kind of person people look up to."

While writing this chapter, a Get-It-Done Guy listener wrote in saying, "I have lost track of that 50,000-foot level, and may have given up on some dreams prematurely or unnecessarily." I know that you, gentle reader, are still deeply in touch with your dreams, so the next few sections will be pure review. Humor me. Identifying your goals and dreams is central to creating a work-less-do-more lifestyle.

Whole books have been written about how to discover or craft your life mission. This isn't one of them. Let's try a few quick hits. If these don't get you going, check out one of the excellent books on GetItDoneGuyBook.com.

We all had dreams as children. Some of them made us wet our beds and wake up screaming in terror. Those dreams, you can leave in childhood. But too many of us also left our inspiring dreams in childhood. We left them in favor of "being sensible." Our dreams don't go away, though. They become a nagging presence, whispering "sell out" every time we meet someone who *is* living what we gave up. Now's your chance to bring that dream back and use it to find a passionate overarching life direction. Start by reconnecting to your dream, as I did. This will help you know where you're going, so you can begin making all your work lead straight to the dream.

As a child living in a traveling New Age commune, I put on magic shows at KOA campgrounds in return for free lodging. I loved performing! And my parents saw how to combine my love of performing with our need for lodging. They had brilliant legal minds, you see; child labor laws don't apply if you don't pay the child. Call it "chores" and they even praise it for giving kids responsibility.

Regardless, I *loved* performing! I really loved it! But then a few years later, I moved into my own apartment and discovered responsibility for real. I was a convert. I put away childish things like magic, went off to get a degree in computer science and then an MBA. By the time I got a good, upstanding job in business, I was so sensible that it *hurt*. And it really *did* hurt.

Deep down, I still wanted to perform. It wasn't even that deep down. At business school, other kids brought slide decks to management communications class. I brought a five-foot satin cloak and used a fake French accent to give my presentation. You'd think I'd have gotten a clue. Nope. I blotted it from my memory. "I must be practical," I told myself. "Performing is too much fun. It will distract me from the serious business of living."

I continued this foolish logic for eighteen years, feeling more and more like I was living the wrong life. It was only after starting my podcast and realizing it gave me such joy that I began to reawaken to my media and performing aspirations.

My dream: to be able to reach and connect with millions of people. Fortunately, it was kind of easy to uncover; the satin cloak was a minor giveaway. Yours may not be so close to the surface.

If you aren't lucky enough to have a suppressed dream tortur-
ing you throughout your day, it's time to ask your intuition or, as
I call it, your Little Voice. Remember, without knowing what you
want out of life, you can't construct a Life Map to help you get
there. And without knowing your purpose, you won't know what
to work less and do more *of*.

Your Little Voice is your source of inner wisdom. It sounds
hokey, and maybe it is, but even an engineer-and-business geek
like me has inner wisdom. You must, too. Our Little Voice knows
what we're about, and when we're making our best decisions. The
velvet Elvis poster you bought, thinking it would look great in your
living room? Your Little Voice knew the truth, if only you'd listened. It's hard to listen, though; it's Little. Most of the time, it's
drowned out by your Big Voice. Let's listen to the Little one.

Grab a piece of paper, a pen, and a calming beverage. As you
sip, quiet your mind. Breathe slowly. Imagine a white cow . . . in
a snowstorm. . . . Ask your Little Voice, "What do I care about so
much I want it to be the direction of my life? What is my highest
purpose?" Then listen. Don't expect anything profound. If it
feels as if you're trying to force your Little Voice to talk, *stop it!*
Just sit still and listen. Eventually it will say something, hopefully
in a language you speak. Write down what it says. *You don't have
to believe it.* You don't have to approve of it. Just write it down.
Then put it away and take a break.

Go do something that satisfies your Big Voice: Play a violent
video game, knit an anatomically correct image of Michelangelo's
David, or call your neighbor and exchange utterly untrue, dastardly rumors about your local city councilman. After your break,
bring out your sheet. Reread it. What did your Little Voice say that
was worth listening to? You're separating yourself from the Little
Voice by time and by writing. You're getting its words on paper, so
they're not trapped inside your head, and you're giving yourself
a chance to enter a new frame of mind before you read them.

Perhaps your Little Voice said something like, "Your purpose is to build a family and home for everyone you love," or "Your purpose is to help save the world by inventing clean fusion" or "Your purpose is to collect a matchbook cover from every dive bar between here and Poughkeepsie." Use that as your dream for now. If it's not quite right, you'll feel it and change it as you build your map.

If you're really stuck, grab a piece of paper and a pencil. Imagine you're talking to the Deity of Your Choice, and he, she, it, or they ask, "Did you live the life I gave you to its fullest?" If you answer no, imagine he, she, it, or they asks the follow-up question: "What would have been a better life for you?" Grab your paper and write down *twenty* answers to the question. Yes, twenty. The first five will be easy. Then they'll get harder. You'll have to dig for the last several. But where are you digging? Through your subconscious mind, of course. Chances are that a couple of the items on your list will strike a chord.

Once you have your list, close your eyes and put your finger down at random. Open your eyes. Congratulations—whatever is under your finger is your life purpose.

Oh, you don't like it, you say? Well, then, cross it off the list. Close your eyes and try again. Keep going until you've found your dream.

Sometimes you'll choose a dream that has some higher-level goals attached, so let's make sure you're really finding your top life purpose. Start with your dream and ask Why. If you still don't have a dream, use "I want to be rich, famous, and have perfect skin." Now ask Why, then take the answer and ask Why again. Keep asking until you get to something so big it's Your All-Encompassing Life Goal. When Michael asked Why, he found he wanted to be a great parent. One more Why and he simply said, "Because that's who I want to be in this phase of my life." When you get an answer like that, you know you're there.

If you're scared to commit, remember *you can change this as often as you wish!* It's your life, after all. Change is normal. When you were eight, you thought living in a giant chocolate-chip cookie house would be the coolest thing *ever*. As you grow up, you learn that chocolate chips melt in the summer and make lousy furniture. Now you want to live in a condo in a full-service building with a doorman who will fetch you chocolate-chip cookies on demand. You are allowed to update your dreams whenever you wish.

(Keep this in mind when you're planning your career. Twenty-year career plans can be dangerous. By the time you're thirty-five, following a plan created by a fifteen-year-old—however well-intentioned—may not be your wisest choice.)

Instead of calling this your Life Goal, we'll call this your Life Vision or Life Mission or Life Purpose. It means the same thing but sounds much more impressive, and will garner secret admiration and envy from listeners when you share it at cocktail parties.

Beneath your Life Purpose, write your career purpose. If you're self-employed, this is the vision/mission of your company. If you're employed by someone else, this is the vision you have for why you're in that job or profession. Since what you do at work is presumably all intended to help the company succeed, its vision becomes your vision while you work there.

Below the company vision are the major goals you're working on to fulfill the vision. You find them by asking, "How can I achieve the vision, given my current resources and environment?" Underneath each major goal, ask, "What projects fall under this goal?" I divide my projects into current projects, future projects in the pipeline, and dreams the Tooth Fairy will grant as wishes (apparently she prefers children, whose teeth fall out naturally. She was quite unmoved by the teeth I left under my pillow. She didn't like the pliers' marks).

Here's my Work Life Map.

VISION

Be Happy!
Help the world be sustainably happy!

↓ academia   ↓ one-man business   ↓ family and home life

↓

SR INC.

Help businesspeople be happier.
Transform business into a Force for Good, Joy, and Sustainability.

↓

STRATEGY

Create a media platform to help large numbers of people challenge and change their relationship to business.	Create information products that help people improve their lives at work.	Deliver coaching and consulting that help people be happier at work and home.

↓

PROJECTS

PRESENT	Get-It-Done Guy Work Less, Do More	E-mail overload Other productivity titles Other series	Sandra C Treeman W
FUTURE	Third-Age expert	Create career product Email overload product	Robert B Scott L
DREAM	Stever TV show Commentator spots Teaching	Permanent distribution or marketing partner so I can focus on creation.	Less coaching, more media. Small # high-paying clients w/ *awesome* goals & challenges.

Even if you believe you don't have separate work and home lives, you have concerns in life other than pure work concerns. Create a second map, but don't put a business mission in the second line. Instead, put whatever guiding principle you may have about who you want to be in your home life.

Now ask, "For each major area of my life (family, work, social, religious), what could bring me closer to my vision that would be fun, motivating, and stimulating to accomplish?" These are your next tier. Under that, list all your projects and activities. Here's my Home Life Map.

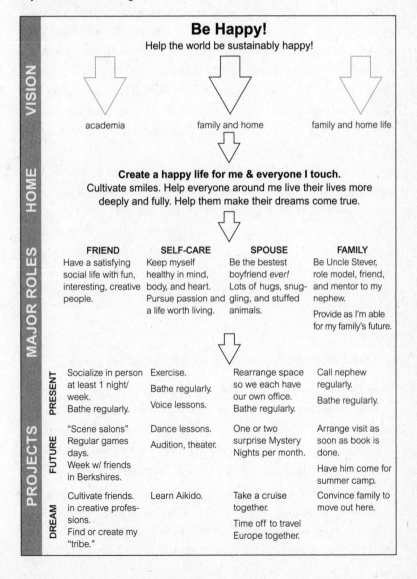

Be Happy!
Help the world be sustainably happy!

VISION

academia   family and home   family and home life

HOME

Create a happy life for me & everyone I touch.
Cultivate smiles. Help everyone around me live their lives more deeply and fully. Help them make their dreams come true.

MAJOR ROLES

FRIEND	SELF-CARE	SPOUSE	FAMILY
Have a satisfying social life with fun, interesting, creative people.	Keep myself healthy in mind, body, and heart. Pursue passion and a life worth living.	Be the bestest boyfriend *ever!* Lots of hugs, snuggling, and stuffed animals.	Be Uncle Stever, role model, friend, and mentor to my nephew. Provide as I'm able for my family's future.

PROJECTS

	FRIEND	SELF-CARE	SPOUSE	FAMILY
PRESENT	Socialize in person at least 1 night/ week. Bathe regularly.	Exercise. Bathe regularly. Voice lessons.	Rearrange space so we each have our own office. Bathe regularly.	Call nephew regularly. Bathe regularly.
FUTURE	"Scene salons" Regular games days. Week w/ friends in Berkshires.	Dance lessons. Audition, theater.	One or two surprise Mystery Nights per month.	Arrange visit as soon as book is done. Have him come for summer camp.
DREAM	Cultivate friends. in creative professions. Find or create my "tribe."	Learn Aikido.	Take a cruise together. Time off to travel Europe together.	Convince family to move out here.

Make Sure Your Life Maps Are Aligned

With goal ladders, we asked Why and How to move up and down the ladder and make sure it was aligned. Your Life Map is no different. Make sure it's aligned by starting at the top and asking "How will I achieve this?" If the next line below isn't your answer, then you know your life is out of alignment. Ask How until you've reached the bottom of your map. In my Home Life Map, I double-check my home vision by asking "How can I create a happy life for me and everyone I touch?" My answers include things like "have a satisfying social life." Those answers are, indeed, what I've written under my "Major roles" line. At least for now, life is in alignment.

Also review your Life Map starting at the bottom. Ask Why for each line. The answer should connect to the goal above. If not, you've found a disconnect to fix. For example, one project on my Work Map is "find a marketing partner." I ask Why and my answer is "to build a successful product business. I bring the content and want someone else to bring the marketing." That matches my business strategy "creating an information products business." Again, alignment!

Use Your Life Maps to Stay on Purpose, Daily

Your Life Maps are your tools for working only on what brings you your greatest goals. They're your broad-stroke goal ladder you can use to keep your life in alignment every day. They help screen opportunities and serve as a daily touchstone to reorient you on what's most important. Life Maps also help surface conflicts that hold you back.

In addition to helping you figure out all your goals, your Life Map will help you decide what *not* to include in your life. When something new and shiny enters your life, your Life Map will tell you where it fits in. Michael's purpose is to be a good parent. If he gets a once-in-a-lifetime chance to spend twelve years staffing an Antarctic research station in complete isolation, he may be conflicted in an agony of indecision. As attractive as subzero temperatures and polar bears may be, Michael's Life Map will quickly show him that it's not for him, at least not without revising his entire life.

My Life Map tells me when to say yes or no so I don't waste time working on something that won't help me reach my goals. Imagine someone offering, "We love your work! Come be the Grand Poobah of our new company making automatic banana peelers. Wouldn't that be fun?" Oh boy, fun! I love fun! My natural tendency would be to say yes! But not so fast.

Where does this fit on the map? It's work, so I pull out my Work Life Map. I start at the bottom and figure out where it belongs: project, big goal, company, or new life vision. Is it a project under a current big goal? Nope. It's not about media, products, or coaching. Is it a new big goal supporting my company vision? Not really; banana peelers don't really make business happier.

If I said yes, this would mean a whole new set of strategies and projects, so the only place this fits is right beneath my life vision, as a whole new company. Is there room in my life for another company? Absolutely not, unless I drop my current company. Sadly for the future of Banana Peelers, Inc., the answer is no. I won't be their Grand Poobah. If I hadn't realized that yes would require rearchitecting my entire life, I might have said yes and ended up with two entire jobs' worth of work! No saves the day.

When to Review Your Life Map

Your Life Map gives you a quick, one-glance overview of your priorities. When you find yourself caught in some activity for a while, glance occasionally at your Life Map and ask why you're doing what you're doing. Maybe it will connect to your Life Map somewhere. Sometimes, it doesn't. Yesterday, I spent hours reading fascinating, gripping, engaging Web sites. Then I glanced at my Life Map. My social-media-addicted brain cried in dismay as I reviewed my Life Map, noting that (big surprise) commenting on blogs is a very low-level activity. Finishing this book is more important in the grand scheme of things. I closed the soul-destroying Web browser and eagerly returned to my manuscript.

Here are some of my favorite times to review my Life Map to bring me back on track:

When surfing the Web, reading e-mail, or doing anything online.   Commenting on a blog about celebrity acne can wait. At least, I'm pretty sure it can.

Before running errands.   Do I really need new boxer shorts right now? Maybe I'll just do laundry, instead.

Making outbound phone calls.   Aunt Sally will still be there tonight. Maybe I can call her then, and make progress on my life during the day today.

Doing administrative stuff.   Filing bills makes me feel so organized! I just love filing! But administrative tasks rarely make progress on my most important goals. We'll learn how to deal with administrivia elsewhere in the book. Your Life Map will get you back on path if now isn't the best time to address envelopes.

As much as I'm sure you want to, you won't always be using your Life Map to link up addressing envelopes or filling out TPS reports with your grand Life Purpose. The lower levels on your Life Map, your actions and projects, are a fine roadmap for day-to-day priorities. When you have five conflicting to-do's and there's only time to do three, look over your Life Map and use it to get a sense of which are more important in the grand scheme of things. Then do those. And when you think "Maybe I should reformat my presentation before giving it," reviewing your Work Life Map will let you return to your priorities, realize another reformatting isn't essential to the survival of the universe, and move on to something more important than changing the fonts in your presentation . . . for the nineteenth time.

When Your Life Maps Don't Line Up, It's Time for a Change

You may find the pieces of your Life Map don't line up. Your big goals may be "Switch to lower quality, lower-cost suppliers" while your Life Purpose is "Produce a masterpiece with everything I do." Or your specific project, "Drop kids at orphanage and take a year off," doesn't match your role as "Faithful, devoted parent." That's how you know it's time to reevaluate. Mismatches make far more work in the end. Your actions will take you far from where you want to be, and later you'll have more work to get back on course. And that isn't including the legal costs involved in dealing with a messy divorce.

As for Michael, a glance at his Life Map was all it took to realize yelling was a crummy way to get Skyler to take responsibility. He was doing tons of useless work banging his head against Skyler's messy bedroom and getting nowhere. In any event, the clean room wasn't even the best way to teach responsibility. Instead, Michael started talking to Skyler about life, and offered his help when *Skyler* was thinking through decisions. One day while talking about dating, Skyler mentioned that a messy room might make a bad impression on a romantic prospect. Michael wisely kept mum.

Now that you have *your* Life Map and know what it is your life's about, use it! Notice when you're wasting time on things that aren't related to your big goals and life purpose. That's work you're doing that's not getting you what you want in life—the very opposite of working less and doing more—of what matters. So stop. Find projects that actually fulfill your purpose. If you spend hours each week volunteering for a nonprofit that gives you no work or personal satisfaction, that's a lot of time working for few results. If your days are filled with meetings that don't help you reach your goals, they're prime targets for elimination. You're just wasting time out of habit. Start using that time for something else. Look at your Life Map, at the projects and dreams that flow from your highest-level purpose, both at work and home. Quit your nonprofit, say no to meetings, and start doing what connects to your real purpose. "That sounds great, Stever," you say, "I'm not feeling superenergetic right now, though. Maybe tomorrow." Er, no. Not tomorrow. Today. Now. Turn the page. In our next chapter, we will tackle that most insidious beast: procrastination.

CHAPTER RECAP

- The best way to work less is to make sure you only do work that helps you reach your goals.

- Your entire ladder of goals and subgoals must be aligned, otherwise you'll waste work.

- Your Life Map, or goal ladder for your life, becomes a way to pull yourself back when you get sucked into the details.

- When the goals and subgoals on your Life Map aren't aligned, you've found an opportunity to choose better subgoals or a more appropriate big goal. Align your goal ladder and your goals will reinforce one another instead of wasting your time, attention, and work with conflicting priorities.

STEP 2

STOP PROCRASTINATING

We all procrastinate, and we put off the very things that are most important. What is *up* with that? When we procrastinate, we do everything *except* work less and do more! If we procrastinated by filling our time with deep, meaningful, soul-enriching activities like spending time with friends, helping children learn skills that will prepare them for adulthood, or bowling, I could understand it. But we don't. We delay what will get us what we want by playing solitaire or restoring our beloved picture of Elvis after humidity has damaged the velvet.

In this "Step 2: Stop Procrastinating," we'll explore how procrastination comes from things under our control, which means the answer to it is also under our control. As tempting as it is to fall back on "Just Do It" running-shoe slogans as the key to success, we'll find that you can set up the world around you to nudge you into action when your brain just isn't up to the challenge on its own. And when the world isn't cooperating, you still have ways to retrain your brain so you'll jump right into action.

Procrastination comes from your thinking. We're going to use the very thoughts that cause procrastination as the keys to overcoming it and sailing merrily along our way.

Let's use me as an example, since I've been procrastinating writing this chapter for two days. And because I'm hopelessly self-absorbed. I glance at my computer, its deceptively innocent screen saver beckoning, "Come to me! Write your book!" Ever the rebellious adolescent, I immediately find reasons to reject my electronic master's seductive command. Thoughts flicker through my mind:

I *have to* work on my book.	Writing isn't fun.
It's such a big project, I'll never finish.	I would rather be out playing.
I have so many *other* things to do.	It won't be any good.
I don't have the resources to pull it off.	People won't respect me if I don't finish.
I don't want to work on my book.	My sweater *really* needs to be de-pilled. Right now.

These thoughts weigh heavily: "I *have to* work on my book." True. And just thinking that sends me into fantasies of all the bad things that will befall me should the work not get done. I imagine my editor, Emily, in full riding regalia atop a gorgeous thoroughbred, looking down at me in pity tinged with contempt. "We had such high hopes for you," she says, as I stand empty-handed in despair. The tragedy of the incomplete manuscript is complete as she turns and canters into the sunset, leaving me groveling wretchedly amid the wreckage of my book. So engaging is the daydream that I don't even remember what I'm putting off.

When you're procrastinating, the procrastination, the excuses, and the daydream are all in your head. If there's that much creativity swirling around in there, why aren't you taking action? Who knows? In fact, who cares? All you need is a way to get things moving.

I'll bet there's a lot you don't put off. Most people shower,

brush their teeth, and get dressed every morning without procrastinating. They just do it. People who cook go shopping weekly
and stock up. They don't procrastinate, they just do it. And when
it comes to putting on shoes and socks, well, gosh darn it, they
just put those socks right on their feetsies and leap into the day.

The difference is thinking. When you think before you act,
you can talk yourself out of anything, no matter how important
it might be.

TURN TASKS INTO HABITS TO STOP PROCRASTINATING

The first step in overcoming procrastination is to turn those recurring tasks you always put off into habits. Think of the things
you do every day or every week that you just do without thinking
about. As for me, I always brush my teeth every day and do the
laundry every week. What makes the things you do on time effortless is *not* their importance. I can survive months without
doing laundry, especially if I don't care about keeping my friends.
Laundry is just not that important. I can get gum infections and
lose all my teeth if I don't brush regularly. Brushing *is* that important. Yet I treat them equally. I do laundry weekly and I brush
daily. That's because they're both habits. Habits are actions we
streamline to the point where they're no longer a decision, they're
just something we do. They don't require thought, so we don't
procrastinate. We just do them.

The easiest way to overcome procrastination is to make things
habits. You can have daily, weekly, monthly, and yearly habits. I
brush my teeth daily, do laundry weekly, pay bills monthly, and
do spring cleaning yearly. That's when I find all the socks that
vanish during weekly laundry.

Establish a habit by making it regular. Put it on your calendar
to remind you. When the time comes, treat it as an appointment.

A solution many writers use to overcome procrastination is to establish a habit of writing at the same time every day, for the same length of time. Once the habit is in place, they just crank out the prose. You'd think I would have established a habit a year and a half ago when I started this book. Yeah, you'd think. If your event in the procrastination Olympics is filling out your weekly expense reports, pick a day and time to do them—say Thursday at ten—and start them every Thursday at ten. Soon you'll be completing these reports as effortlessly as you brush your teeth before bed. If you don't make your tasks a habit, you're stuck back with your thoughts, which can derail even the simplest of tasks. Potential habits to develop: checking and responding to e-mail only at specific times, working out, grocery shopping, balancing your checkbook, getting together with friends (perhaps for a regular Sunday brunch), cleaning the living room, doing laundry. At work, you can build habits around straightening your desk, writing regular status reports, checking in with people you're building relationships with (which I'll get to in step 8), offering to help your teammates, following up on prospect calls, touching base with customers, and meeting with your manager or the people who report to you.

USE BABY CHUNKS

Sometimes the tasks we procrastinate are big, one-time projects, so turning them into habits just won't work. Procrastination experts say to break these big projects into tiny chunks and use baby steps to move forward. The first time, I misheard this as "take baby chunks." The visual was so disturbing that I knew I had to invent a real technique to go with this memorable instruction.

Taking baby chunks isn't about breaking your project into pieces, it's about breaking *time* into pieces. When there's an end in sight, it's easy to buckle down and power through. That's why we like speed dating. We'll even talk to someone who doesn't floss when we know we can move on in a mere three minutes. When a task seems endless, we're terrified, because deep down, we fear getting trapped. Marriage has no end point; meditate on that and despair.

With baby chunks, you'll speed date the task you've been procrastinating. Set a time limit (preferably with an actual physical timer) and work 100 percent for that much time. Then get up and do something else. From the moment you sit down, you'll know that in just a few minutes, you'll be free once again.

When I first began writing, I would write for ten minutes and play games for fifteen. I played more than I wrote. But it gave steady progress in ten-minute chunks. Every hour included twenty minutes of writing. Over a day, that added up to almost three hours.

Over time, I shifted the balance to include more writing. Even so, short chunks of time with a defined end point let me relax enough to get going when the job seemed overwhelming. You can use the same technique for mind-numbingly boring things like planning business trips. When you have travel to book, meetings to set up, hotels to reserve, and details to juggle, you can do it ten minutes at a time. Spend the top of each hour comparing fares on a dozen Web sites. By day's end, you'll have devoted an entire eighty minutes and be ready for your very first excursion to Sheboygan.

Now we know about baby chunks and habits. Let's make a habit of baby chunks. If you're procrastinating several projects at once, each project becomes an excuse not to work on the other. Report due tomorrow? No time to work on it; I have to work on my taxes. Taxes due tomorrow? But I really *should* work on my report. You need to make sure you're doin' chunks with all your projects, or else the one that's not moving forward will become the siren that seduces you away from the others.

USE DAILY ACTION PACKS

A Daily Action Pack* is the answer to keeping track of all your projects. A Daily Action Pack tells you what you need to do daily to guarantee progress toward your goals. You can choose a certain amount of time to spend on each project, as we did with baby chunks, or you can choose some other way to decide a good day's contribution. Let's say you work for Tasty Munchies, Inc., and have to review the monthly financials from your forty retail stores by the end of the month, twenty days from now. (For some of us, this would be the most boring thing *ever*. For you, it's a thrilling expression of your life's true purpose.) You must review forty reports in twenty days. That means, you must review two reports per day to make your goal. You know if you read your two daily reports, you'll finish the project.

Gather your major projects and figure out what daily dose will be enough to move each project forward. It might be a number of pages to write or read, a number of phone calls to make, or a certain amount of time spent each day on a project. Write these all on your Daily Action Pack. What you'll end up with is the minimum needed to move everything forward. And you calculated it knowing if you do it daily, you will eventually finish everything.

Now that you've created your Daily Action Pack, make it a habit. Every day, pick it up and make sure you run through every item on the list. You will keep everything moving, and if you do it first thing every day, you know you're done for the day as soon as you have finished your Daily Action Pack—even if the whole thing only takes half an hour.

---

* Thanks to Scott Wintrip and Jay Perry of jayperry.com, cofounders of the Simply Effective coaching program in which I was first exposed to the Daily Action Pack.

CREATE A WEALTH INVENTORY

One of my favorite ways to procrastinate is by whining. No matter how reasonable my baby chunks are, I can always whine to convince myself to do something later. My favorite whine is, "I don't have what it takes to get this project done." And gosh darn it, I'll stretch reality to the breaking point when I'm whining. I've postponed a project for hours after whining that I didn't have quite the right pen. I needed a .38 mm bright blue, gel ink pen. And since I can't stand listening to whining, I'll do anything to shut me up. In this case, it meant a trip to the stationery store. Yes, I actually have a codependent relationship with my own procrastination.

When you feel like you don't have what you need to Make It Work, think again. Though you couldn't bring a book to your high school finals, life is an open-book test. You have a lifetime's worth of help, if you remember to use it. The best way to remember is to write it down.

What are *your* life resources? You know people, you have money and things, and you have skills. At any moment, you think of one or two of these at best. But if you make a wealth inventory, you can jog your memory whenever you need. You never know when your ability to act out Poe's *The Raven* interspersed with Seuss's *Horton Hatches an Egg* will be just the thing you need when preparing your presentation on the quarterly numbers for the actuarial group.

Get out a piece of paper. Write four column headings: people, money, stuff, and skills. Under each column heading, write in the people you know, your money, your stuff, and your skills. When filling in people, scour your address book. Write down anyone you could ask for help: high school friends, college friends, teachers, bosses, and that strange-but-nice relative with the peculiar skin condition you met at your family reunion. Write them all down.

In the money column, list your cash, and anything that could be turned into cash. List assets you could borrow against, credit cards, and all the ways you could get money if you absolutely needed to. We're not saying you're going to use any of these resources, just that you have them available.

In the skills column, write down everything you're good at. Sometimes you'll find you have skills you can apply to a problem in really creative ways. When you're postponing a project by bemoaning your lack of resources, get out your wealth inventory. Browse it. Ponder, pontificate, explore, think, and research. Bring it all to mind and let your mind begin to make connections to figure out how you could use what you already have in getting the job done. Your wealth inventory helps you get going again when a challenge seems daunting.

When a start-up company was searching for a way to highlight its product, the marketing manager found himself very busy doing anything but approaching potential marketing partners for a product launch. He didn't know any likely partners off the top of his head, and he was scared to cold-call. Then he reviewed his wealth inventory. A resource was an old directory of trade shows from a former job. Seeing that sparked the idea of contacting his city's department of commerce, finding a current directory, and adding promotional speeches and product booths to their launch strategy.

If only I had really looked over my wealth inventory when procrastinating by whining about not having the right pen. What would my wealth inventory have told me? Under "skills," it seems I can write with *any* writing implement. Who knew? Under "people," I know Brent, the pen counter czar at my local stationery story—it's only a block away. I could ask Brent to bring a pen by during his lunch hour. And resources would be the most embarrassing. I'd have to face the two hundred pens I already own and tell them why I don't love them anymore and am looking for a replacement. That would be really tough, especially since I would have discovered I already *have* a .38 mm bright blue, gel ink pen. And maybe surveying my inventory would have gently reminded me that I don't need a 201st pen; I can just start writing.

USE OTHER PEOPLE

Sometimes, even with baby chunks and all your resources lined up, you need to call in the big guns: other people. When other people are counting on us, we're hard-wired to perform. We give it noble names like "accountability," but underneath it's really just us being scared Mommy won't love us if we don't do what we say. Using other people is also an excuse to create a shared bond with our other friends who are procrastinating, too. Not to mention having fun sniping together at the few who don't have the courtesy to procrastinate, and are actually going to the gym, or meeting all their deadlines. For me, involving other people is about friendship and fun, so it immediately makes the task I need to complete more engaging. And there's a deeper reason that bringing along a friend can help you get started.

When we know someone else is expecting us, we feel compelled to live up to the expectation. Social scientists have done all kinds of research showing this is true, even if your parents *didn't* use the meat hook punishment when you were young. This makes friends extra helpful when setting up habits. Make an appointment to call your friend every day at the time you want to establish your habit, say "I'm reading through my Daily Action Pack and planning my day" (or whatever habit you're trying to start), and then listen as he, she, or it does the same in return.

Once you've got your friend hooked on helping your habits, you can expand your check-in to a more sophisticated version that moves *all* your goals forward. I learned this from coach Andrew Thorn. In the *New Manager 101* course, which doesn't exist, thus accounting for the sorry state of management in the world at large, they say, "What gets measured, gets managed.*" When you created your Daily Action Pack, you created measures. You chose a number of pages written per day, or a length of time spent, or a number of phone calls that you would consider real progress. You can use the measure for your Daily Action Pack; you can also use it as, well, a measure of progress. Next, enlist a friend to help you track your measurements. You'll find yourself making amazing progress when you combine accountability with measurement.

First, you need a friend. Any kind will do. If you don't have one, make one from scratch or use a mix, that's what social networking's all about. You can also use the same one you used to help create habits. Make sure it's someone you trust and can talk with daily.

Next, you each get out your Daily Action Pack and look at the measures you chose for it. You can also include measures related to any other goals you might have. Make each measure a number or a yes/no question like "Did you throw away at least one old expense report today?" Measure the actions to reach the goal, not the goal itself. So for sales, don't use a measure like, "How many sales did I make?" Use a measure like, "How many new prospects did I find?" "How many prospects did I follow up with?" "How many existing clients did I call to discover other products they might need?" . . . things like that.

---

* Your brain learns things based on feedback. There's a whole body of science behind the relationship between feedback and action. I'm not going to talk about any of that here, though. Instead, I'm going to rely on trite, overused management buzz phrases. Aren't you happy you bought this book?

Now set up a five-minute daily meeting. Your friend asks you about each of your measures. Answer honestly. Then switch, and you ask your friend. All you do is ask for the measure, with a supportive attitude. No criticism or judgment allowed; only support and encouragement!

A sample session might go like this. My goals are to write this book, clean the apartment, and sort through the pile of mail by the front entrance hall that's grown teeth and is munching on my sneakers:

FRIEND How many pages did you finish today?

STEVER Three

FRIEND How many minutes did you spend putting things away in places where they *really* belong?

STEVER Fifteen

FRIEND How many pieces of mail did you handle?

STEVER Eighteen

That's all there is to it! Your friend listens supportively. This is purely about accountability and measurement. You find where you're sticking to your goals and where your efforts are falling off. You don't even need to ask your friend for help. You're smart; given the right measurements, your brain will automatically help you change. What makes this work is having accountability from someone who also offers unconditional positive support consistently. Do this daily if you really want the benefit.

USE ACTION DAYS

Daily check-ins with a friend give you a regular reminder of your current projects and actions. Then it's your job to actually do the work. Sometimes, though, even the best of intentions and tons of feedback aren't enough to get started. Even knowing daily how many pages I wrote the day before, it can still be a huge challenge to sit down and write. But if one friend can help keep your whole life on track, surely a *dozen* friends can help you get going on your daily tasks!

And yes, there is a way to have an incredible day with a group of friends: action days.* You'll get a lot of action, that's for sure. Here's how they work.

You and a few friends get a conference line. They're free, they're everywhere, and they're wicked useful. I include links to a few on this book's resource Web site. You agree to check in at a certain time each hour. For example, right on the hour.

At each check-in, someone (you?) reads the attendance list. Each person *briefly* reports what they've done in the last hour. Then they promise the group what they'll do in the next hour. Once everyone has reported, you get off the phone and go for it!

Here's a sample:

STEVER   In the last hour, I've coached a client and designed a workshop for MBA students on why not to get an MBA. In the next hour, I will call my agent, make soup for lunch, and write a blog post.

AL   I've written the executive summary of my report. In the next hour, I'm going to rehearse it for half an hour. If it's all good, I'll print the handouts and send them for duplication.

PAT   I taught my chihuahua to sing harmony. In the next hour, I'm going to build a miniature of the Taj Mahal out of toenail clippings, recite *The Raven* while meditating in Tree pose, and write a proposal for my dissertation.

---

* I first learned about action days through the life coaching community. Specifically, Thomas Leonard, who pretty much invented the field.

This brings up an important point: It's fun to invite a variety of people. You learn how different people's lives can be. But no judgment, please. In an action day, you're providing accountability for one another. If your friends have weird goals, well, this is your chance to get to know them a little bit better.

Resist the temptation to chat. Stay focused on making things happen. No group therapy here. When Sally says that in the next hour she's preparing a memorial service for her recently deceased pet cockroach, don't follow up. It's not your place to question why she feels the need for a memorial service. And you really don't want to get into why she was emotionally bonded to a pet cockroach in the first place.

Action days are especially good for things that are tough to start. Some things I've done during an action day include: writing a book chapter, updating a Web site, designing a class, cleaning my office, processing a backlog of bills, reading reference material, emptying my inbox, replacing lightbulbs, fixing a leaky faucet, and planning travel.

MOTIVATE YOURSELF

When other people aren't around, you have no choice but to motivate yourself. To get yourself moving, find something about your situation that *does* excite you enough to commit. You may love your industry or your company most, and that love will carry the day. Many people who work in nonprofit or government jobs are motivated by the service they are providing for others. When the director of a nonprofit that delivered medical care to homeless people contemplated cold-calling potential donors, he was often tempted to procrastinate out the wazoo. Reorienting on his company's mission motivated him to pick up the phone and kick-start his fund-raising season.

USE YOUR LIFE MAP TO GET MOVING

If you're putting something off, ask yourself why you're trying to do it in the first place. Remember your Life Map from step 1? Good. Because it's the quickest way to connect to your highest motivation and also make sure the task you are procrastinating is worth doing in the first place. Get out your Life Map to find out which project or action on your Life Map is driving your need to do the task. Then look at the higher levels on your Life Map, taking a few minutes to connect your Task to Be Done with your higher goals and purpose. Maybe you took your exciting job as an actuarial accounting consultant to save up enough to retire for life in six years and are now procrastinating the presentation you have to make to the partners in your firm. Even if you hate presenting, counting down days to retirement can motivate you to find a way to make progress. And being an actuary, you can even know if the odds are in your favor of living until that age-forty retirement!

I'm using this method right now. When writing gets tiresome—and *jeez*, can writing get tiresome—I remind myself how neat it will be to have a book in print—one of my higher goals on my Life Map. And on the publicity tour, I plan to be discovered by a Hollywood agent and cast in a recurring role as "engaging geeky neighbor #4" on a top-rated TV series—another higher goal. The dream is what keeps me moving.

Knowing the link between your task and your motivation for doing the task is good information, but not always enough to turn into action. You can't just tell yourself, "I must do my taxes to fulfill my project of having an organized house. That will meet my high-level goal of being a good homemaker, which is a key initiative in my Life Purpose of building a family empire that will conquer and enslave 68 percent of the world's population."

For one, it takes too long. But more subtly, statements don't force you into action. And of course, sometimes there will be tasks that you just absolutely have to complete, regardless of how they relate to your Life Map.

This is when asking yourself questions can help. The right questions not only lead us to answers, but can lead us to action. What happens when someone asks you a question? You feel *compelled* to answer it. In fact, you probably thought about the answer to *that* question as you read this very paragraph. If questions trigger automatic action, let's design some questions to get us moving.

Build yourself questions about the action you need to take. They can involve all the elements we've discussed so far. You can ask about the task itself, about baby chunks, about your passion, and about involving other people. Here are some of the questions I used to get moving on this chapter:

What's the smallest chunk I can finish that I'll feel good about?   Answer: Outline the chapter. I did it, then took a break and went to the gym. I've used this question a lot, and more and more, the answer is, "a paragraph." It seems like such a small thing that I can almost always get myself to sit down and write just a quick little paragraph. . . . And after five or six of those, I've written a page. You can adapt this question for whatever task you're doing. If you're cleaning your office, how many items can you put away to feel like you've made progress? Throwing a party? How many balloons can you inflate in one breath? The possibilities are endless! (So how many do you need to investigate in this particular sitting?)

What's the funniest image I can come up with to work into the chapter somehow?   Answer: Emily with a riding crop, with me groveling at her feet. When I get a really funny image or idea, I want to capture it while it's still fresh in my mind—this gets me writing. Of course, this only applies if you're doing something funny. If you're writing a report for the board of directors, you might ask, "What's the most important thing we've done in the business this year?"

All of these questions orient my mind to create new, fun content that will move my writing further along.

Here are some sample driving questions and the underlying principle I used to create them:

PRINCIPLE	QUESTION
Link your task to something more enjoyable.	How can I make my taxes fun?
Use baby chunks.	What's the smallest piece of my report I can write that will still be progress?
Involve someone else. Implied accountability (since we'll have to compare notes at the end of the hour). Friendly competition.	Can I get more done in the next hour than Joel?
Time limit, so there's a light at the end of the tunnel.	What can I accomplish in just 15 minutes?
Action day accountability. (The phrasing of the question kind of gives it away, doesn't it?)	What will I tell my action day partners at the top of the next hour?
Connect to passion around team/industry/company values.	How will the team celebrate when we've brought this project in on time?
Tie my task to larger, inspiring dream.	What will I tell Oprah when she asks for procrastination advice during my book tour?

Once you've created a set of questions for yourself, start asking them. When you're sitting across the room, curled up on the couch reading a book, staring at your computer, not-filing-your-expense-reports, just stop. Take a deep breath and begin asking your questions. "How great will it feel to have this totally behind me?" "How long would it take me to process just one receipt? Just one?" Keep asking until you stand up and begin working on your formerly postponed task.

WHEN ALL ELSE FAILS, USE CARROTS AND STICKS

When all other ways of taming your brain fail, you just might resort to bribery. Reading the news, it seems like they use it for politics, in banking, and for high-level corporate negotiations. Why not use it personally, as well?

Halfway through writing this book, some friends were going out to a movie. I politely declined. "I must stay home and work on my book." Yet as time went on, boy, did it sound like more and more fun to join friends at the movies! So I told them, "If I make it through five pages by the time the movie starts, I'll join you tonight."

That was an hour and a half ago. I just made it through five full pages of writing—in two hours, that's a frickin' awesome accomplishment. All I did was amp my want-to through the roof. When I wanted to finish badly enough, everything else fell away as I charged ahead.

Self-bribery is most powerful when the bribe expires. My friends were going to a movie, and not getting done in time meant I would miss them. The movie time wasn't negotiable. The deadline brought everything into crystal clarity. Expiring bribes can include plays, movies, parties, and anything scheduled. You can also arrange for a bribe to expire. "If I'm not done with my budget numbers by six p.m. tonight," you happily tell your best friend, "you can have the last piece of my Oreo ice cream cake. Otherwise, I get to eat it." As long as your best friend loves Oreo ice cream cake, you've just added a deadline to your bribe.

Gluttons for punishment can turn the motivation all the way up to eleven by pairing rewards with punishments. If you don't finish your budget numbers by eight p.m. tonight, you have to clean the litter box and take out the trash for a month. But if you finish before five p.m., you get a wonderful sushi dinner. Then invite friends to the sushi dinner. Now you have social pressure to finish by five, and punishment pressure to finish by eight if you miss the earlier deadline. It's amazing how many budget numbers you can crunch when your prepurchased tickets to the World Wrestling Federation's *Wrestlemania* are on the line.

PAY ATTENTION TO YOUR PROCRASTINATION

Sometimes your procrastination could be an important message from your own brain. A coaching client called for help revitalizing her business; she just couldn't motivate herself to work on her business plan. Then events outside her control caused the funders to pull out their money, forcing her to shut down her company. She was ecstatic! Only when it was gone did she realize she hated her job and wanted out. No wonder she'd been having trouble. When your unconscious mind wants out and your conscious mind says "stay," the conscious mind rarely wins. When you're ambivalent about a goal, you fight it even while trying to reach it. This isn't a recipe for success; it's a recipe for that horrible pudding your mother used to force you to eat. If there's a task you can't stop procrastinating even with all the tools we've covered, it might be time to listen to your brain and evaluate what's really going on.

Overcoming procrastination is an adventure that will bring

you closer to the world of working less and doing more. Since we procrastinate by doing low-priority, unimportant stuff when we *should* be doing what's important, postponing stuff guarantees we're working ineffectively. Getting right down to work isn't always easy, but it's worth the effort to reap the rewards.

CHAPTER RECAP

- Procrastination comes from thinking.

- Turn regular recurring tasks into habits. Bypass thinking and you bypass procrastination.

- Work in baby chunks, small time blocks where you go in seeing the other side.

- Create a daily action pack to keep multiple projects moving forward steadily.

- Use a wealth inventory to get past the "I need outside help" blocks.

BRING IN PEOPLE

- Check in with a friend to help each other create a habit.

- Monitor daily progress with a daily check-in buddy.

- Have action days with friends. (Or see the book resource Web site GetItDoneGuyBook.com to find others for action days.)

TACKLE YOUR OWN THINKING

- If you aren't passionate about the job, reconnect to your passion about the tasks, industry, company, or life purpose to get you moving.

- Use questions to kick yourself into action.

- Bribe yourself.

STEP 3

CONQUER TECHNOLOGY

Where are my robots? They said we'd have robots. When I was growing up, in the not-too-distant past, we still had a hazy, rose-colored notion that technology would liberate us to work less and do more. The future always had robots. They would understand my every command, vacuum, sweep, pick up after me, pour me a cocktail before meals, and be my best friend. Every episode of *The Jetsons* promised.

Well, it's the future. Robots *do* exist, doing jobs people used to do. The people? Surely they're reclining in their space chair, drinking space martinis, driving their hovercrafts to Mars, and living the Good Life. So why am I still waiting for the robots to liberate *me* into a lifetime of leisure?

If you're still waiting for the robots to liberate you, this is your chapter. Technology is marketed with a pure "work less, do more" promise. Does it deliver? We'll expose the dark, sordid truth to the cleansing light of day. With our new, clear insight into Universal Truth as it applies to technology, we'll make sure that our technology is really helping us make our Life Maps come true.

If anything, technology has helped us work more and do

less.* Technology certainly *changes* how we do things, but it often makes less work in one area while making much more work in others. And it's expensive, requiring more work to pay for the cool technology that helps us work less.

We have high hopes for our technology. Unrealistically high. Cell phones and laptops were supposed to deliver us to a paradise of days spent in parks, where work was a mere afterthought in our deep, meaningful lives. As if! Our corporate masters instantly saw that technology wouldn't turn our work lives into play, but it was a fabulous opportunity to turn our play lives into work. Now, even our vacations are tethered to the job. Our cell phones isolate us in public, and they've become the biggest driving danger since the screw-off cap on a fifth of gin. I recently visited a country where people use technology less. They were weird. They sat in cafés, moved their lips, and waved their hands around. They called it "hanging out with friends." It looked like a lot of fun, and certainly better exercise than typing on a cell phone.

In *The Wizard of Oz*, Glinda asked Dorothy, "Are you a good witch, or a bad witch?" We should ask that a lot more often. Technology can be both a good witch and a bad witch. If you're using it to reach the highest goals on your Life Map (which may involve working more efficiently), it's good. When it diverts you from reaching your highest goals, it's bad. When it diverts you while pretending to help you, it's worst of all. You can make technology your personal good witch by making sure it fulfills its purpose. In this chapter I'll help you first evaluate your technology to make sure it's actually working for you, and then I'll give you all kinds of work-less-do-more tips for your computer, e-mail, and assorted devices.

---

* Make no mistake, our corporate masters have found technology very, very useful. Since they get the benefits of our work, they *love* technology. I'm talking about the effects of technology on our daily lives.

TEST YOUR TECHNOLOGY TO MAKE SURE IT DELIVERS ON ITS PROMISE

Why do we need technology? We think it will make our lives better. But rather than thinking, "If I use this technology, life will be better," think, "If I use this technology, life will be *different*." Then decide if the difference is worth keeping and if it will actually help you work faster.

After buying my first handheld PDA, I resolved to spend an entire year running my life entirely from the PDA. My PDA and I celebrated our one-year anniversary by reviewing whether it delivered on its promise:

To-do list.   Fail! It took more time to add items, and items that got pushed beyond the first screen or two never got reviewed or done. Paper was faster to write and scan, and it forced me to review my unchecked-off list every time I filled up my notepad. Besides, my paper had perfect handwriting recognition, and my PDA didn't.

Calendar.   Mixed. Having my calendar in convenient ones and zeros made it easier to coordinate with my assistant. Huge win! But I kept overscheduling in weird ways. Because my handheld couldn't show me a week or month with any detail, I tended to rely on day view. In day view, I couldn't get an overall sense for how to balance my life. I would schedule a seven a.m. meeting the morning after a late-night party and not realize the conflict. Unexpectedly, the synchronization screws up about once a year, requiring hours of work to fix it each time. When you add that into the mix, it's probably better to keep my calendar completely offline. Due to my geek-guy fascination with technology, I choose *not* to add that into the mix and my calendar is as online as they come. Don't make my mistakes.

Address book.   Win! I can add notes to people's address book entries. My address book gets copied online and offline, and shared with my assistant. It's only gotten better over time. Now you can include pictures, so when the notes field says, "Spent a fabulous week together in Palm Springs," you can recall *which* fabulous three-week companion this was; memory gets so much easier when you're sober.

Now that I know which technologies work for me, my life is perfect as perfect can be. I keep my to-do list on paper. My calendar is online where I can view month-at-a-time on a big screen, and it syncs to my handheld. And my address book is completely online. I didn't assume technology would meet my goals; I tested it out!

I wish I could give you a guaranteed set of guidelines around technology, but I can't. Your job, when you finish this chapter, is to hold your technology to standards. Decide why you use the technology you do. Test it out and evaluate it ruthlessly to make sure it's living up to its promise. If not, let it go free.

For the rest of this chapter, I'll share how I tame specific technology to ensure it makes my life paradise on Earth. Even if you love what I do, don't just willy-nilly adopt my habits. Remember to make sure your technology is serving you before you touch it. Efficiently using technology that isn't getting you what you want is just streamlining ickiness.

CONQUER YOUR COMPUTER

Computers sparkle, glow, and give us political news. They add little to our lives in a deep sense, but give us the *illusion* of engaging with life, without the inconvenience of actual muscular movement. All it takes is a fourteen-pound bag of M&Ms, an intravenous drip of Coca-Cola, and some microwave popcorn, and we might never have to leave our desk.

Your computer likes your undivided attention. When I think of the years spent in front of a computer, rather than out in the real world, I want to weep. I get so depressed, I visit Web sites on overcoming depression. Then I play violent video games to express my rage at all those wasted years. Before long, there I am, in front of my computer, ignoring the fact that my life sucks because I'm sitting in front of my computer. I am nothing if not consistent.

I'm sure that *your* relationship with technology is healthier than mine. You use your computer as little as possible, only to get essential tasks done, and then you get up, and engage in healthy, face-to-face interaction with people. No? If not, it's time to reconnect with your computer, but only in a healthy way.

Rather than making her the center of your work or home life, use your computer as a tool. A really fun, useful tool, but a tool nevertheless. You get tools out when you need them and put them away when you're done. And you don't use them for random stuff. You use your jackhammer to break up concrete, and then use your mixer to make a protein shake. You don't try to make the shake using your jackhammer. Or if you do, it only takes a single try to realize what a *really* bad idea that is. Some relationships improve with a little bit of breathing room. You'll get much more done—and love your computer much more—if you spend some time apart.

Most offices are designed so when we sit down, we're at our computer. Change that! Move your computer physically away from the center of your desk. If sitting at your desk means automatically facing your monitor, you'll get snagged. If you put your computer across the room, using it requires conscious thought.

Next, *schedule* your computer time! When you think you need a computer, don't use it right away. Keep a paper list of what you need to do during your computer time. For example, the list might contain several items:

- Return Bob's e-mail.
- Upload the draft of the Web page.
- Read the report that Sandy sent.
- Spend fifteen minutes on my favorite news site to catch up on the world.

Keep your tasks distinct and specific, with defined endpoints. If your task is "surf the Web," add a time limit so you know when you're done.

Now you know your computer time schedule. Get up, walk to the computer, and do one task. When you finish, stand up and step away from the computer. Get something to drink. Remind yourself the task is done. Put the tool down. Then come back, do the next task, and so on.

You can also use an egg timer or stopwatch to remind you to step away. You might find this trial separation turns your computer from an involuntary lifestyle choice to a genuine productivity tool.

The same goes for your laptop when you're traveling. My best business trip ever was when my laptop hard drive crashed as I was leaving for the airport. In my computerless-for-two-week trip, I rediscovered thinking, taking paper notes, and paying attention to the world around me. My work quality soared.

Leave your laptop home for holidays, too. Your laptop pulls you away. That beautiful, seductive creation of crystal, titanium, and plastic beckons. It says, "You can catch up on work for just a couple of minutes before taking that hot tub, relaxation massage/ yoga class." Resist the siren song! If you absolutely need to access something on it while you're gone, use remote-control software from the lobby in your holiday resort (see the resource Web site for links to such software). Every computer platform in existence has it, now. You'll have to wait in a long line in the business center, as people walk by, pointing and laughing at you, subjecting you to endless ridicule and contempt from your family for being a slave to your computer. With enough humiliation, you'll learn to resist temptation and spend time with your loved ones instead.

You kept a list of your computer tasks after moving your computer away from your desk to help you stay focused. When you're using your computer for research, you'll be voluntarily diving into a hyperlinked maelstrom of interesting information that can suck you in for days. Keep a sticky pad by your computer. When you're getting ready to do research, jot down on the pad the three or four questions you want to answer. Then dive in and start researching.

Nine hours later, you'll see the note out of your peripheral vision as you're just finishing up an important online quiz about your favorite celebrity and liposuction. "That's right," you'll think, "I sat down to research brownie recipes for the upcoming team pot luck" and you'll zip right back to your preexisting agenda.

Make sure to take the sticky note down once you're done, though. If you leave them around, it's possible to start taking them for granted and ignoring them. You want them to stay novel and fresh, so toss 'em when you're not actively using them.

CONQUER VOICEMAIL

Different companies have different cultures. In some places, voicemail can be a huge problem. In other places the problem is e-mail. I'll be telling you how to deal with both, but you'll need to decide which one wastes most of your time as my voicemail solution involves using e-mail, and taming your inbox might require voicemail. The question of which is your biggest time suck—e-mail or voicemail—may even change. That is okay. Just use my e-mail tips when you want to chuck your phone across the room and use my voicemail tips when you want to drop your computer out the window.

If you find your time, effort, life energy, and soul being sucked away by excessive voicemail, you want to subjugate it to your will as soon as you can and this section is for you. Don't get me wrong; voicemail is a great technology. It lets someone who isn't even present bore you to tears when you have other, important things to do. Instead of interrupting you in person, people can do it using technology. While e-mail and instant messages can be quickly scanned, voicemail takes time to listen to. This is a potential landmine for us who want to work less! Someone outside our control has just put us at their mercy by controlling how much time we have to listen. They can monopolize our ear as long as he, she, or it wants. We say, "Please leave a brief message after the tone." They ramble on for fifteen minutes.

Some evil callers decide they don't like leaving voicemail and will only talk to us live. If they call a lot, they can make our lives a living heck. We need to tame voicemail users, including ourselves!

Create a Better Outgoing Message

There's no reason your outgoing message should just say "Leave a message." Use it to set expectations with your callers, right up front. Tell people when (or if) to expect a return call. Callers must listen to your whole outgoing message, so keep it brief. If there's a key callers can press to skip your message, start with that:

Hello, this is Stever. Press # to skip this message. I check voicemail at breakfast, right after lunch, and at four p.m. Please leave a message and I'll get back to you soon.

When people leave a message, we feel compelled to answer. It would be rude not to. We believe we must respond or at least justify ourselves. We think, "If I don't respond, they'll think I'm a jerk." Or, "They'll fire me." Personally, I go straight for the endgame: "If I don't respond, they'll despise me. They'll burn down my home, steal my stuffed tiger, kidnap me, and leave me in an alley, covered with envelopes, to die a slow death by paper cut."

We *know* our callers won't do as we ask. We ask them to "please leave a brief message" and they just won't do it. Why should they? They do what they want and we accommodate them. Yes, we complain, but we give them what they want and they don't have to change.

And then, we feel like *we* owe *them* a quick answer? If I were a psychologist, I might use terms like *abandonment issues* or *codependent*. I'm not, so I'll just tell you how to end this way of thinking.

First we must embrace our hatred of voicemail and put those feelings to good use. Call your own mailbox and rant to yourself about how much you despise those incoming messages. Really let it all out. Until, that is, you've filled your mailbox completely. Then have your outgoing message say "Please e-mail me." People will find your voicemail box full, and will have no choice except to e-mail you. They can still reach you, but on your terms.

If you can't fill up your voicemail box, find out if you can set it to give an outgoing message only. In the worst case, disable it entirely, or leave an outgoing message saying, "Please don't leave a message. This voicemail never gets checked." Use the passive voice for that last sentence and they'll never notice *you* are the one who decided not to do the checking.

For the persistent caller who insists on talking live, you can always take the phone off the hook. Only put it back on when you're ready to take calls. You can also use caller ID or "call intercept" to screen on a caller-by-caller basis. If your "friend" decides not to leave a message, that's their business, not yours.

You might think you have to take calls from clients, bosses, or polyamorous family units. Nope. Just 'cause they're a client doesn't mean they can interrupt! *Never* answer the phone if you're doing something that takes concentration, like writing, or trying to solve the last level of your favorite video game. Let calls go to voicemail or let them send an e-mail, and then deal with the messages later.

"But," you cry, "how will I explain myself to people?" That's another myth. You don't actually have to explain anything; just talk about what you'll do. "I'm not picking up the phone today. I'll check voicemail at a breaking point. Or, you can keep trying to call back." Or, "I'm not checking voicemail, though I am checking e-mail." Then smile honestly and sit quietly. Now the ball's in their court.

If someone has the poor taste to insist on an explanation, say "because." You can say anything afterward, it really doesn't matter. "I don't answer because I'm not picking up the phone right now." "I'm not taking voicemail because my mailbox is full."

If these don't work, blame the little voices. You do have little voices, don't you? "I don't answer because the little voices said not to, and I always do what the little voices tell me." If they persist, widen your eyes, frown slightly, and say, "Wait . . . the little voices are telling me something right now . . ."

Seven Rules for Leaving Voicemail

I know it's hard to imagine, but sometimes you'll call someone and they won't pick up, so *you* will have to leave a voicemail. Be careful! If you leave bad voicemail, you'll need more follow-up phone calls before you get what you want from the other person. That's working *more*, not less.

Of course, sometimes it saves work to call and leave voicemail when you know a way-too-chatty Bernice is out to lunch. For *our* convenience, leaving voicemail is just nifty. A few simple guidelines will help you leave a voicemail that gives you the greatest chance of concluding your business quickly, efficiently, and without having to talk to another human being as long as you live.

It's great for those awkward conversations. "Hey, Billy, loved the artwork. We can't use it, but thanks for the three weeks of free work," or "It's been a great relationship, but I've met someone who'll support me *and* do the dishes. Toodles!"

1. Always leave your full name. "Stever, tag, you're it! Couldn't reach you, so am hoping you'll call me back. Have a great day!" She sounds friendly, too. She's even waiting for me to return her call. Unfortunately, I have no idea who she is!

I can't say this enough. Leave your full name. *They'll recognize my voice.* No, they won't. Leave your full name. *But I'm leaving my message for my parents.* That's nice. Leave your full name. Your parents agonized over that name. They almost divorced while debating *Filligan v. Dormalia.*

If you're breaking up with someone via voicemail, definitely leave your name! Don't be so self-centered you believe they'll know who it is. You've been cheating, maybe your shmoopie has, too. If you don't leave your name, you might put your shmoopie in the awkward position of not knowing which of you is breaking up.

2. Always leave your phone number twice. "866-WRK-LESS." Once at the beginning and once at the end. *But they have my phone number!* you cry. Not in front of their eyes, they don't. Just leave it at the beginning and end of the message. If they miss it the first time, they'll have a second chance. And whether their voicemail has "rewind ten seconds" or "replay from start," they'll quickly be able to get right to the number with only a couple of key presses. "866-WRK-LESS."

3. Speak slowly and clearly. Your brain screens out traffic, conversations, and wind while you leave a message. You hear the dulcet strains of your own voice, while the voicemail system hears static, wind, the occasional siren, and that truly disgusting belch you expelled without a second thought. Oh, yeah, and your cell phone is cutting out while you leave the message. Speak slowly and clearly.

4. Leave enough information so the person can take the next step. Don't just say "Call me." Tell them enough so they can proceed without calling back, or if they call back, they can do it having made all the progress possible. "This is Oskar, calling about the, er, health issue. Could you call me back with the name of that antibiotic? And what's your favorite cotton swab? Thanks!"

5. If you're just calling to touch base, let them know when they can call you back. There are times you want a phone call, and times when you don't. Since you *will* turn your cell phone off during a romantic dinner with your shmoopie, tell your voicemail victim, "Give me a call today after three, tomorrow at seven, or Thursday between nine and noon." You'll help them and save your love life, all at once.

6. Keep it short and simple.

7. Make it fun. Make your voicemail easy to listen to. Be humorous. Sing. Deliver your message in rhyme. I do all these things, and people love getting messages from me. If you're going to force people to think of you, have 'em think of you fondly.

If you remember nothing else, remember this: leave your name, repeat your number, speak slowly, and carry a big shtick.

CONQUER YOUR E-MAIL INBOX

If you solved your voicemail problem by telling people to send e-mail, you've just shifted your load from one inbox to another. But at least your overload is conveniently in one place, at this point. Now you just need a simple way to deal with your e-mail inbox.

Probably the most common twenty-first-century ailment is e-mail overload. Once upon a time, it cost money and effort to send a letter. That made it work, so people activated their brains before sending something off. E-mail is so quick and easy that your coworkers, spouse, and kids can just dash off an e-mail asking you to do something, and *they* feel they accomplished something. They're wrong, of course, because when one hundred people *all* delegate their problem to you, you simply have a nervous breakdown, drop out of society, change your identity, and live out the rest of your life walking along the beach in Maui. Throttle that e-mail and regain your sanity!

Check E-mail at Defined Times Each Day

Don't let e-mail interrupt you! We hate telemarketers during dinner, so why do we tolerate e-mail when we're trying to get something useful done? Turn off your e-mail autocheck and only check e-mail one to three times per day, by hand. Let people know that if they need to reach you instantly, e-mail isn't the way. Just asking them to exert the effort to pick up a phone and press buttons to call you will eliminate about 80 percent of your incoming e-mail in one fell swoop.

Some of the people who care enough to keep contacting you

will call. But if your voicemail message tells them to e-mail you, they'll get caught in an infinite loop forever calling and e-mailing you. Save them from this fate by deciding how they really *will* be able to reach you—phone or voice—and letting them through.

I use voicemail as my contact of last resort. My e-mail tells people to call if it's urgent. If they call, they get my voicemail if I'm unavailable. But my voicemail greeting does *not* tell them to e-mail! It just says I'll call them back. When I'm available again, my voicemail is the first to get checked.

Just as your voicemail greeting sets expectations for callers, you can use your e-mail signature to set expectations for people you e-mail. You're only checking your e-mail a couple of times a day, so tell people that, so they don't expect an instant response. E-mail programs let you set up a signature that gets added to outgoing messages. Include your e-mail policy in your signature. Mine says: I only check e-mail once per day. If you need immediate response, call!

If you respond to e-mails right away, you train people to expect your immediate attention, and they'll oblige. On the resource Web site, you will find walk-throughs showing you how to set the signature on many popular e-mail programs.

Respond to E-mail More Efficiently

Part of the problem with e-mail is that you read it online, where you can also act on each message the instant you get it. Every few seconds, your attention will be yanked to and fro by the agenda of whoever's e-mail just happened to arrive. Cut that link by not responding immediately until you know *all* of the work on your plate.

Grab a legal pad and label it "Response list." When you check your e-mail at your predefined times (one to three times per day), run through your incoming e-mails. For each, note on the paper what you have to do or whom you have to call. Don't respond immediately, even if it's a quick "under two minute" response. Keep focused on going through your inbox! If there's important reference information in the e-mail, drag it to your *Reference* folder. Otherwise, delete it. Zip through your entire list of e-mails to generate your response list. *Then,* zip down your response list and actually integrate your responses into your normal task management routine.

If people are using e-mail to load their work onto your shoulders, if you have the power, hit right back and shift *your* need for sushi dinners onto *their* shoulders. One CEO I've worked with charges staff members five dollars from their budget for each e-mail she receives. Amazingly, her overload has gone down, the relevance of e-mails has gone up, and the senders are happy, too, because the added thought often results in their solving more problems on their own.

If you are constantly copied on things you shouldn't be, begin replying to e-mails that aren't relevant with the single word: *Relevant?* Of course, you explain that this is a favor to *them.* Now, they can learn what is and isn't relevant to you. Beforehand, tell them the goal is to calibrate relevance, *not* to criticize or put them down and encourage them to challenge your relevancy as well. This is the same principle we saw with our Life Maps. We're working less by working *only* on what's most relevant.

Sometimes people send e-mails that are just too long. When someone sends you a ten-page missive, reply with three words, "Yup, great idea." You're working less, and everyone around you is learning not to expect huge answers from you. Then you can answer at your leisure in whatever format works best for you. My favorite format for long answers is dictating my answers to an assistant who types them up while I recline in a bubble bath with a glass of champagne and Kate Bush playing in the background. Sadly, I don't have a bathtub, can't afford champagne, and Kate

Bush lives in another country and doesn't like to fly. So usually I just settle for the three-word e-mail.

Another way to prevent a constant barrage of e-mails that await your response is to type your response directly, but schedule it to be sent out in a few days. That works great for conversations that are nice but not terribly urgent. By inserting a delay in each go-around, you both get to breathe easier and you train people to not expect a quick response, which will lead them to only e-mail with the important questions—not the more trivial ones that will waste your time. See the book's resource site for instructions and resources to help you send out delayed e-mail.

Just Ignore It

Another way to deal with a full inbox? Ignore it. Yes, ignore e-mail. If something's important, you'll hear about it again. Trust me. If e-mail isn't your preferred method of communication decide how you *want* to be contacted and let them know. People will gradually be trained to pick up the phone or drop by if they have something to say. This tip is for those people who don't have voicemail problems and so won't mind getting these messages if it means a lighter inbox. (If you don't want to be contacted at all, you can train people to ignore you. It might not be great for your career, but with proper meditation and chanting, solitude might help you reach enlightenment.) After all, if it's not important enough for them to tear their gaze away from the hypnotic world of Microsoft Windows, it's certainly not important enough for you to take the time to read.

Achieve "Inbox Zero" So Easily Your Head Spins

There's been a lot of talk about achieving "inbox zero." That's a mythical state in which your inbox is empty. Excuse me if I snort cynically. If you ever manage to empty your inbox, you simply have to wait five minutes and it will be full again. The question is not how to empty your inbox, the question is how to process it quickly as stuff comes in.

Here's how you keep an empty inbox:

> Select all the messages in your inbox.
> Delete them.

You're done. You think I'm kidding? I'm not. You can declare a mini e-mail bankruptcy for the week. Based on an idea by Lawrence Lessing of *Wired* magazine, you delete everything. Then send a form letter to everyone who wrote saying, "My backlog was too big to manage. To cope, I've deleted everything. Please resend anything important." If you're afraid you would seem less manly-man by admitting weakness, you can skip the reason and use flattery instead. "Your e-mails are so very important to me, would you be a dear and resend any important e-mail?" Of course, that phrasing has its own manly-man problems. . . .

If you're like me, you have nightmares thinking of deleting unread e-mail. Shadowy e-mail messages dance through your dreams wailing, "How could you abandon me?" Get over it. Most of your e-mail just isn't that important. I'm a one-man shop, so I know what's important: about 5 percent of my e-mail brings in cash or helps me get work done. Everything else is free to be nuked. What about nonwork friends who e-mail? Simple. I read their messages but actually catch up by phone after work. Soon they're trained not to e-mail me.

You might be scared you'll insult people by not responding. Maybe, but maybe not. Everyone's inbox is overflowing and they'll often cut you slack. Everyone, that is, but your high-strung friend Bernice. Bernice will take your silence as a personal attack on her integrity, her choice in clothes, and her worth as a human being. If you spot a Bernice in your inbox, just reply. It's easier. Sometimes you don't know which of your friends is a neurotic time bomb, waiting to blow. If someone loses it because you ignored them, just apologize profusely and be as gracious as possible.

You can't declare e-mail bankruptcy every day; people will start to question your commitment. That's fine, just don't declare e-mail bankruptcy. But keep on deleting everything. If you're doing it daily, however, add one more step:

Open your "Deleted items" folder and rescue any messages you think you absolutely *must* deal with.

Most of us go through our inbox and decide what to delete. Here's how our brain copes: "Look at all this stuff I have to do. Everything I delete represents me dropping something on the floor, so I have to be really careful about what I delete." Your brain does something very different when you're rescuing messages. It thinks, "Hey, my inbox is empty. All this deleted stuff is off my plate, and *I* get to control what I bring back. Let's be really picky."

If you start with one hundred messages in your inbox and delete the irrelevant ones, you'll probably end up with twenty to deal with. At three minutes apiece, your inbox just handed you an hour's worth of work.

If you trash all one hundred messages and rescue the important ones, you'll probably end up with about five to deal with. At three minutes apiece, you turn an hour of work into fifteen minutes. That forty-five minutes you bought back adds up to five weeks per year.

Delete-and-rescue cuts through the noise and gives you just what's most important.

Finally, you can take steps before traveling so you won't have a backlog when you return. Some e-mail providers let you set a vacation message that gets sent to anyone who writes when you're away. Have your message say you're away, you're deleting everything when you return, and people should resend important messages when you return. Don't promise to read your backlog or get back to them later! You can't control whether your backlog will be manageable.

Send Better E-mails

Aside from taming your inbox, you'll also want to make sure you're not wasting time composing e-mails. Because e-mail is electronic we think it must be fast. We're so wrong, it hurts. Typing more than a few words takes a wicked long time. I'm typing eighty thousand, I should know. Yes, it's faster than handwriting, but it's much slower than talking. When your e-mail hits three paragraphs, pick up the phone and call. Just keep the conversation brief.

The phone gives you more rapid conversations. So instead of spending an hour typing that three-page e-mail, you can spend two minutes giving the same information by phone. Just keep it focused and don't drift off into gossiping about the latest plot twist on *General Hospital*. (Hint: They'll never resolve it. The show's been on for generations, and they've *never* resolved it. Gossiping won't help.) As we saw, knowing how to leave good voicemail can speed your voicemail exchanges. The same is true of e-mail. Since we send a lot of it on any given day, we can work less by streamlining how we compose and send e-mail. We can also write an e-mail that makes it so easy for the recipient to respond that our back-and-forth is nearly instantaneous.

Turn Spell-Check Off

My simplest tip for writing e-mails more quickly involves spell-check. I send a lot of e-mail. When typing "in the flow," writing furiously, my misspelled words conveniently highlight with a red squiggly. Now I get to stop and decide whether to correct the word now or later. It's a tiny interruption, true, but it derails my flow, just a bit. Over time, that adds up, and so I suggest turning off your spell-check. That's right: turn off your spell-check.

I discovered this trick by accident when the spell-check-as-you-type setting somehow got turned off in my e-mail program. My concentration improved and my e-mail composing went much faster. My e-mail program now spell-checks all at once before sending a message, so I can put my full attention on my spelling once composing is done. It's made so much difference that I even turn off my spell-checker in my word processor when writing memos, speeches, presentations, or books. For those, however, I must remember to run the spell-check manually before printing my final draft.

Summarize Your Message in the Subject Line

You'll get the quickest response to your e-mail if your recipient can reply without even opening it. Seriously. When you write your subject lines, use the subject line to summarize your message. Don't *describe* your message, *summarize* it. For example, if you're sending out a message about the staff meeting being rescheduled for next Thursday, a subject line of "Staff meeting" is useless. It tells people nothing.

A subject line, "Staff meeting rescheduled for next Thursday" is better. People know the key information from the subject line alone, and can decide whether or not they need to read the whole message.

Better still is, "Staff meeting rescheduled for Thursday, January 21, 2012." E-mail can sit around for weeks in someone's inbox. "Next Thursday" or "two weeks from now" or "the end of May" means something different depending on when the message finally gets read. If you include references to time, make sure you include the actual date or time. Just in case.

When your subject line is a good summary, people can quickly deal with it and get back to you. But not every message can be summarized in the subject. Sometimes you need someone to take action, schedule a meeting, or do something that requires a bit more work. The secret is to compose your e-mail body so you give them enough information that they can make all the needed decisions and reply to you with a reply that handles everything.

Include All Your Scheduling Information

You'll most often be discussing time when using e-mail to schedule meetings with people. We've all done the Scheduling Agony Dance. Let's schedule a one-hour meeting. It will be simple:

ME   Are you free tomorrow? I'm free tomorrow.

THEM I'm not free tomorrow. I'm free Thursday.

ME   I'm not free Thursday. How about Friday.

THEM Great, two p.m.?

ME   No, I'm busy until two.

THEM Oh. I'm busy after two. How about next Monday?

You can short-circuit this by putting all your scheduling information in the very first message. That way, you need at most one back-and-forth:

YOU   Are you free tomorrow? I'm free tomorrow, Friday after two p.m., Monday all day, and next Wednesday through Friday.

You just saved you both hours of time you can now spend relaxing in the office hot tub.

Include Enough Context So They Know What You're Talking About

And for goodness' sake, don't start your messages with an answer—"Yes! I agree. Apples are definitely the answer"— without offering context. Your recipient must read seven included messages, notice that they were copied, and try to figure out what apples are the answer to. Even worse, they don't really know if they should care. Oops! There are *ten* messages people have sent about apples. One of the others says "Apples are definitely *not* the answer." And another says, "Didn't you get my message about apples?" But which message was sent first? And which was in response to which? ARGH!

It's very, very difficult to get to the core of the issue.

You're probably sending an e-mail because you're deep in thought about something. Your reader is, too, only they're deep in thought about something else. Even worse, in a multiperson conversation, messages and replies may arrive out of order. And no, it doesn't help to include the entire past conversation when you reply; it's rude to force someone else to wade through ten screens of messages because you're too lazy to give them context. So, start off your messages with enough context to orient your reader.

BAD E-MAIL:
To: Billy Franklin
From: Robert Payne
Subject: Re: Re: Re: Please bring contributions to the charity drive
Yes, apples are definitely the answer.

GOOD E-MAIL:
To: Billy Franklin
From: Robert Payne
Subject: Re: Re: Re: Please bring contributions to the charity drive
You asked if we want apple pie. Yes, apples are definitely the answer.

Answer Your Reader's Questions Before They Ask

Including your context and scheduling information in a message is just one example of the general principle of answering questions before they ask. A little more up-front work will save hours later.

Put yourself in the mind of the person you're sending an e-mail to. Ask yourself what questions they might have about your message. Then answer those questions before they ask. Be brief and organized! Not only will you be doing them a favor, but you'll get better at writing a really useful e-mail knowing how your e-mail will be used.

For example, if you're collaborating on a paper with someone and you want to send a bunch of references you found on the Web, you could just send a list of URLs pointing to the articles you think are useful. And what will they do with that information? They'll likely want to visit the articles and find out which are relevant to the part of the paper they're writing.

Since you already have the pages open in your Web browser, you can cut and paste the titles of the papers into the message along with the URLs. Then your reader can quickly decide which links to follow,

Make Action Requests Clear

If you want them to follow a link, do research, or take some other action, please tell them! Remember, you want to go home early. Even the most worshipful admirer of yours won't be able to deliver what you need quickly unless they know you're expecting something. If you want things to get done, say so. Clearly. There's nothing more frustrating as a reader than getting copied on an e-mail and finding out three weeks later that someone expected you to pick up the project and run with it. Summarize action items at the end of a message so everyone can read them at one glance.

Separate Topics into Separate E-mails . . . Up to a Point

If someone sends a message addressing a dozen topics, some of which you can respond to now and some of which you can't, send a dozen responses—one for each topic. That way, each thread can proceed unencumbered by the others.

Do this when mixing controversy with mundania. That way, the mundane topics can be taken care of quietly, while the flame wars can happen separately.

BAD MIXING OF ITEMS:	GOOD MIXING OF ITEMS:
We need to gather all the articles by February 1st. Speaking of which, I was thinking...do you think we should fire Sandy?	**Message #1** We need to gather all the articles by February 1st. **Message #2** Sandy's missed a lot of deadlines recently. Do you think termination is in order?

Combine Separate Points into One Message

Sometimes the problem is the opposite—sending five hundred tiny messages per day will overload someone, even if the intent is to reduce this by creating separate threads. If you are holding a dozen open conversations with one person, the slowness of typing is probably substantial overhead. Jot down all your main points on a piece of (gasp) paper, pick up the phone, and call the person to discuss those points. I guarantee you'll save a ton of time.

Compose Using Templates

The physical act of composing a message can also be streamlined. If your job involves answering lots of inquiries, for instance, you may spend much of your day typing polite chit-chat and fancy e-mail signatures. If your coworkers are forgetful dorks who are too lazy to find their own answers, you may end up answering the same question over and over and over. That means more typing.

Stationery, also called a template, is a completely prewritten e-mail message. A macro is a character or short word you can type that magically turns into a much longer sentence or paragraph. And signatures are things like, "Sincerely, Jane," that get added automagically to the end of every message.

Stationery is useful when you have a lot to say and you say it often. If you get the same question over and over, set up stationery with the answer. Next time someone writes in with that question, call up the template, change a few words to fit their situation, and send it off. If you work for a politician, you could prepare stationery with standard replies for common issues. You might have one template that addresses "The mayor's position on traffic lights for children." Or you could have one template to reply to people who want traffic lights, and another template for people who like watching kids dodge cars as they run across the street.

If your concern is the polite chit-chat at the start and end of messages, you could set up stationery with all the polite chit-chat in place and type into the middle of the letter. Or, you could use macros.

A macro is a keystroke or short set of characters that turn into something longer when you type them. Let's say your boss has you saying no to a dozen different requests each day: a dog show invitation, a request for money, and someone claiming to be a long-lost child, asking to be added to the will.

These are pretty different. You want to respond to each individually, but your responses can have paragraphs in common. All might start like this: "Mr. Boss appreciates your letter. Your tragic plight is touching." Then you add a paragraph or two crushing that person's lifelong hopes and dreams, and you finish up with,

"Mr. Boss regrets that he can't do more for your deeply troubling situation."

What you do is define a macro so you type "opening" and it turns into Big Boss's statement of appreciation. You define another macro so you type "wrap-up" and it turns into the paragraph on regrets. Then to type the full letter, you just type "opening," the custom paragraphs, and "wrap-up," and there it is!

I use a macro so I just type GIDG and it turns into "The Get-It-Done Guy's Quick and Dirty Tips to Work Less and Do More." That way I can mention my show by its full name and save my fingers for more important things, like picking the pretzels out of a snack mix.

Signatures are just what they sound like: "Sincerely, Senator Duzzalot." You set a signature in your e-mail program and it gets added to every outgoing message. You'll never have to type "Sincerely" again. Depending upon your boss, this could save your integrity.

The specifics for setting up stationery, macros, and signatures depend on what computer and e-mail program you use. Search your help file for the words *stationery, templates, macros,* and *signatures* to find the details. This book's resource Web site also has instructions for using stationery, macros, and signatures in some common e-mail programs.

CONQUER YOUR PDAS

Turn the darned thing off. Just turn it off. Just as you schedule your e-mail time, schedule your PDA time. Otherwise it will eat into everything you do, destroy your relationships, cause you to crash your car, and turn your brain into a mindless pile of mush. If something is important enough to warrant interrupting your life, it will still be there when you get home to your computer.

BE A SMART TECHNOLOGY BUYER

One of my final tips for conquering technology is to be a smart technology buyer. You'll be dazzled at how much time and money you think your new gizmo will save you. Put the dazzle on hold and become Sherlock Holmes for a moment. Ferret out all the hidden costs that come with your technology: upgrade costs, supplies you must refill (ink cartridges, toner, memory cards), cables, batteries, et cetera. Also consider if the technology really works and you depend on it, how much trouble will you be in if it breaks down? Will it be a big disaster or a minor inconvenience?

Technology often breaks down. Many people ignore it. "I just lost seven years' worth of research when my hard drive crashed. I guess that's life." You may choose to do something about it, but beware of the temptation to fix problems yourself. You'll happily think it will take twenty to thirty minutes to find a problem . . . and two days later, you're still struggling with it. You bought your technology to help you work less and do more, and now you're working more trying to keep the technology working. As a general rule, if I've tried for more than three hours to fix a broken widget, it's likely to take me days to fix it on my own. After three hours, I take it to a service center or, if it's a computer, wipe the hard drive and reinstall my system from scratch. Remember: The issue isn't whether you can fix it, the issue is that your time-saving technology is now eating up your time in the form of maintenance frenzy.

CHAPTER RECAP

- Don't assume technology will help. Know why you're using it and actually reflect to find out if it's fulfilling its purpose.

- Try out the various tips in this chapter for taming your technology. Most of the tips involve finding ways to separate yourself from your technology and not allow *its* interruptions to set *your* agenda.

- You can always turn it off. If necessary, by using a hammer. Then you can call your tech support people and say, with complete innocence, "I keep pressing the on button and nothing happens. . . ."

STEP 4

BEAT DISTRACTIONS TO CULTIVATE FOCUS

The human brain works best when you're totally into what you're doing. You go with the flow, and the flow carries you to Doing Great Things. Focus is the skill that will help you find and follow the flow. Once you're in the flow, nothing seems like work. Whatever you're doing seems effortless, and you do great things with incredible ease and grace. But of course the world doesn't make it easy to focus. That would deprive you of a tremendous opportunity for spiritual growth as you try to focus and find it nearly impossible.

In the modern world, the upper hand has been grabbed by Focus's nemesis, Distraction. You can't focus unless you first have ways to deal with distraction, which is where this step comes in. Most of this chapter will offer you a way to get your mind and body into a laser-focused state of get-it-doneness worthy of a Constitution-class starship at Warp 9. But first, you need to get your distractions under control. Otherwise, they'll kill your focus, destroy your warp drive, and reduce you to running on impulse engines. That would be bad.

BEAT DISTRACTIONS WITH AN INTERRUPTION LIST

When distractions intrude, *don't* drop everything and chase them; triage. If there's a true emergency, of course you drop everything and handle it. Little Stephanos got his ear caught in the rice-picking machine, again?* Off to the plastic surgeon, pronto.

But mostly, what the universe needs from you can be put off a little longer. Grab a piece of paper and write in nice, neat letters at the top, INTERRUPTIONS. This is your interruption list. When an interruption rears its ugly head—and the head *will* be ugly—jot down the interruption on your interruption list. Now you've dealt with it! Wasn't that quick and easy? You can keep working, secure in the knowledge that the would-be distraction has now been dealt with and is safe and secure on your list.

Life would be wonderful if that really were the end of the distraction. But it isn't. At some point, you have to deal with the interruptions. Let's be logical. If interruptions take time, and we schedule time, then we must be able to schedule interruptions.† And sure enough, it's easy. Choose a block of time, preferably late afternoon, perhaps four p.m. Schedule a half hour for "interruption catch-up."

Jot down the interruption "Bernice needs help with medical details for our forthcoming do-it-yourself Siamese Twin Separation kit." Say to Bernice, "I'm busy right now. How about if I get back to you a little after four p.m.?" When your catch-up time arrives, run through the list and handle the interruptions.

---

* Come on. You know I like the original *Star Trek*. The rice-picking machine was sure to show up at some point.
† Clever use of tortured logic, eh? It's called "junko logic." Think of the relationship possibilities.

Interruptions depend on what you're doing. If you're a taxi dispatcher, your life is a gazillion interruptions every second. Nothing's an interruption, because your job is to deal with *everything* as it happens.

Interruptions also depend on where you are. A singing telegram is an interruption during a romantic dinner with your wife, husband, spousal equivalent, or polyamorous family unit. But it might be a welcome break at work, if you're preparing for a board presentation.

Some jobs get many, many interruptions. Service organizations have constant new demands coming from every side. You may need multiple interruption times. You defer interruptions to the time block that seems most reasonable.

Some interruptions aren't very urgent and needn't be done the same day. A client of mine, a senior executive in charge of evaluating new training programs for her company, scheduled Fridays as her "interruption day." People would bring some cool new program she just had to check out. She loved trying new things, and would say yes every time. Gradually, the interruptions became overwhelming and she spent most of her time evaluating new programs.

Her solution was to schedule an interruption day. When new ideas came in, she would lovingly save them up for Friday. When Friday arrived, she pulled out all the programs and had a great time getting paid to frolic through her playground of programs and try them all out.

SET BOUNDARIES TO PREVENT INTERRUPTIONS

Most distractions come from those loving, caring beings we call "people." They pretend to be polite, and even to be our friends. But we know deep down they just want to absorb our life energy for their own purposes. Since we don't yet have robots to deliver our message for us, we have to set those boundaries ourselves. That can be a challenge as many of us have a pathological need to be liked, so we put other people's agendas ahead of ours. We're also primates who worship hierarchy, so we put the boss's agenda *way* above our own. But consider this: There may be three competent bosses in your company who know their job is to make *you* successful. They fully support helping you work as effectively and efficiently as possible. They understand that your deferring them to your interruption time means you're really getting stuff done. Sadly, your boss is not one of the three, so you routinely destroy your own productivity so you can run down to the closet to fetch her white Hermes scarves. And yet, if you spend all your time supporting your coworkers, you'll never get your own work done. If your boss is who interrupts you the most, sit down and say, "Interruptions break my flow enough that they really tank my productivity for the hour. Would you rather I be immediately responsive to your IMs, or would you rather I work in the zone and check my inboxes a few times a day at defined times?"

If your boss isn't mature enough to hear that, then they do not understand their job and you should expect them to be promoted to executive sometime in the next six months. If your boss is competent, however, it should lead to much improved working conditions during your boss's remaining three weeks at the company.

When setting your boundaries, be polite and respectful! When someone pops by and says, "Hey, let's go to lunch," screaming "You bonehead!! How could you interrupt me when I was just about to write the climactic sentence of my expense report? I hope you burn in Heck!" is not going to win you any friends . . . except possibly your cell mate, when you're locked up for assault.

Use a calm, gentle tone. Frame your message in terms of *your needs* and *their benefits.* "In order to bring 100 percent of my time and attention to helping you, I need to be able to bring 100 percent of my time and attention to other issues when I'm working on those." Then tell them of your boundary, whether it's deferring their emergency to your interruption time block, or only answering e-mail at predetermined times. Then shoo them away gently. If you told them you would get back to them later, enter that in your interruption to-do list or in your calendar, whichever makes sense.

People can be taken aback by boundary-setting, since it's rare in modern life (feel free to buy them a new copy of this book to introduce them to the idea). But if you're polite and firm, they will honor your request, and deep down, they'll secretly admire your fortitude and strength of will.

Learn How to Say No

Okay, boundary setting isn't always as easy as I make it out to be. That's because we get tripped up saying no. While saying "Yes, dear" may be the secret to the perfect romance (if you mean it), sometimes your real answer is still no.

The ultimate boundary protection is saying no. Too many yeses overcommit us. You can never work less if you can't say no. You'll just say yes to more than you can handle, overcommit, and never, ever catch up. Period. It can't be done. Yet most of us have a very hard time saying no, especially to our boss. "Miss my kid's soccer game because you screwed up the schedule again? Sure boss, I'd love to."

Why do we do this? If you're going to be in a soul-destroying codependent relationship, why do it with your boss? Choose someone you love—like your snuggle bunny—to make you that miserable. A better choice is saying yes to yourself. Protect your boundaries! Only take on work you can handle. And say no when someone asks you to go past your limits.

I know you're thinking "If I say no, I'll get fired. My family won't love me. Other kids won't play with me. I'll have to join the carnival and eventually die alone behind a carnival popcorn stand, smelling of booze, still wearing my red nose and oversized clown shoes." Yes, it could happen. And if you say yes, you'll overcommit, lose your family, lose yourself, and live alone in a cubicle, smelling of mouse pads, still wearing your powder blue shirt and undersized khakis. It's your choice. Sure, saying no has real consequences. It's just that saying yes does, too. We're often way too scared of the consequences of no, and not nearly scared enough of the consequences of yes.

If it's your boss asking, you can just say, "My plate is full. Let's review my projects and decide what to change so I have time to add something." Then, review and reprioritize. Just make sure the new priorities get added to the objectives for your yearly review.

Saying no doesn't mean you have to get angry, defensive, or unpleasant. You listen fully to the other person. Acknowledge what they've said, and then say ". . . and no." The best no-sayer I've ever heard is Byron Katie. Here's how she demonstrated saying an honest no.

I'm playing the role of Katie's boss, asking that she skip some family time for work.

s   Hi, Katie! I know it's three o'clock Friday afternoon, but I just remembered I need the TPS report by Monday morning.

k   Actually, I can't. But I know there's another way. Why don't you call . . . so-and-so.

s   Oh, but Katie—I need you to do it.

k   I hear that, and I'm unable to. Merry Christmas.

s   Surely, you could just do it tonight, after dinner.

k   Actually, I'm unable to. I can't.

s   This is going to show up on your annual review.

ĸ I hear that, and I think that's a very honest thing to do, because in reality, that's correct.

Now, a coworker asking for a favor.

s I have a hair appointment at lunch. Could you cover for me at
the desk?

ĸ Actually, I'm unable to.

s Oh, come on. I'll cover for you next time.

ĸ I really appreciate that. I'll look forward to that for sure. And
I'm unable to cover you on this one, but I know you'll have
a great time at the hairdresser.

s You're not being a team player here!

ĸ It really looks that way, doesn't it? And of course, as we know,
I am.

Finally, a teenager who wants to borrow the car.

s Hey, Mom! Can I use your car to go to the movies?

ĸ No, sweetheart.

s All the other kids' parents let them use the car.

ĸ That's true. We really have different lives.

s If you loved me, you'd let me use the car.

ĸ It's so interesting you'd say that. I love you with all my heart,
and I'm not letting you use the car.

s Mom, I hate you! I hate you! Everything in my life that's wrong
is wrong because of you.

ĸ Oh, honey. I'm so sorry you feel that way. I adore you.

What doesn't come across in print is the voice tone and warmth
of Katie's answers. There's no defensiveness, hostility, or hesitation.
Visit this book's resource Web site to hear the original audio inter-
view. Her answers are simple. She doesn't argue, justify, get angry,

or get sarcastic. And she doesn't back down. Note especially that she doesn't get sucked into the "Why not?" discussion. There's no reason to go there if you're truly committed to your no.

Remember: Sometimes you need to say no to interruptions so you can say yes to your current commitments. Listen deeply, acknowledge the other person, and then say no from a place of kindness. Your no will protect your boundaries, repel the distraction that comes from interruption, and help you focus on

USE TECHNOLOGY TO BEAT DISTRACTIONS

Interruptions force us to lurch from project to project as each incoming interruption redirects our attention. We'd *all* be happier if everything about a given project happened all at once, all in one place. When we decide it's time for that project, we go to the One Happy Place* to work on the project.

Here, technology can come to the rescue! Punt distribution lists and e-mail. Instead, use collaboration software to create a central hub for shared files and documents. You won't have to e-mail drafts of documents back and forth. Instead, put them in the shared hub and everyone can grab 'em at will.

As for e-mail, choose a tool with a message board. Rather than a gazillion e-mails, just post your questions, concerns, and status updates to the message board. When you want to concentrate on the project, you just visit the hub and see everything related to your issues in one quick scan.

Even better, choose a tool that lets you e-mail your messages directly to the collaboration board. Then you can still indulge your illusion-of-instant-gratification sending of e-mail, but your teammates only get the response when they are ready to pay attention. It's all very win-win. Visit the resource site for links to some collaboration tools.

---

* This is different from the One Happy Place we retreat to when having surgery, being tortured, or sitting through a boring meeting.

getting into the flow that helps you get stuff done easily—and quickly.

STOP MULTITASKING AND START FOCUSING

Once you've protected yourself from outside distraction, it's time to start focusing. That means doing one thing and doing it well. It's the exact opposite of the workstyle everyone worships these days: Multitasking. Multitasking is all the rage. Workers do it. Managers do it. Daddies do it. Mommies do it (supposedly better than daddies). I hear people proudly proclaiming their incredible multitasking skill. It's become more than a habit; it's an identity.

If you're doing sixteen things as you read this, believing you're mastering all of them, you're actually probably doing a mediocre job at every single one.

That's why multitasking won't help you. At *best*, multitasking is no better than monotasking. At worst, multitasking makes you do less and work more, but you *feel* as if you're more productive. Some people think they can do several things at once, as long as they're so good at each thing that it requires almost no mental effort. Like, say, having a conversation while you're driving a car. Even though both require very little conscious thought, every study shows that talking on a hands-free cell phone while driving reduces your reaction time as much as drinking and driving. Multitasking "automatic" tasks doesn't work.

It's also multitasking when you switch activities quickly: for example, if you work on a report for a little while, then pay bills, then answer e-mail, then work more on the report. Sometimes you can do this and be superproductive. Other times, you get far *less* done. In both cases, of course, you *feel* like you're accomplishing a whole lot. And wouldn't it be nice if your feelings had anything to do with reality.

"But I *like* to multitask!" you cry. Of course you do. And I like to listen to showtunes and dance around the living room in my underwear. I just don't expect to accomplish very much by doing it. The research (which is quite extensive at this point) says nothing about whether you *like* to multitask; it says when you do, you do a poorer job. You may be happy doing a poorer job in exchange for the adrenaline rush. That's cool; multitasking *feels* very exciting and productive. And it *is* exciting, just not very productive.

Cameron Gott, a coach who works with people who have ADHD, makes a great distinction. He writes that many professionals believe they are excellent multitaskers. Not so. They may be excellent multireactors, managers, and responders, but not taskers. They don't complete creative products. That requires focused attention, energy, and resources. Monitoring social media and responding in sound bites isn't multitasking, it's multitending. When something noteworthy comes through a channel, *then* the multitender pays attention.

If you want to multitask in the sense of completing multiple creative projects at once, you need to start by realizing a truth about multiple projects: Switching between projects many times a day is slower than doing all the work you can do on one project, then all the work you can do on the next project, and so on.

Imagine two five-hour tasks: preparing a marketing report (M), and writing a deployment document for your Ghoul-based Authoritarian Initiative (G). You work one hour on the report, then one hour on the deployment, and alternate until each task is done. After ten hours, you will be done with both. As of hour eight, neither task will be done. At hour nine, the marketing report will be done. At hour ten, your GAI deployment will be done.

If you do the tasks one after the other, you work on your report for five hours. Then you work on your GAI deployment. At
the end of ten hours, once again, both tasks are done. But your
report gets done after five hours. Working sequentially, you have
results much sooner than if you multitask.

In a perfect world, multitasking still gets your report and deployment plan done at the same time. So why worry? Because
this example assumes you can switch between the two instantly.
In practice, you can't. It takes time for your mind to reorient.
And who switches straight from marketing to Ghouls? Not me! I
put down my marketing manuals, very satisfied that I've done a
whole hour's work. Before starting the Ghoul deployment, I decide
to check tomorrow's weather report. And run to the bathroom.
And drop by Thaddeus's office to chat. And say "Hi!" to Carol.
And . . . six hours later, I come back to continue with my deployment report.

Different tasks require different information and maybe even
physical locations. It takes time to make the change. You can lose
up to 40 percent of your productivity every time you switch tasks.
So if you multitask, your report and deployment plan will likely
take you fourteen or fifteen hours, not just ten. You will feel like
you've done much more work, however, because you spend so
much time and mental effort switching.

When you're focusing, you do one thing at a time. Just one.
People try to cheat. I'm sure *you* would never say something like
this, but I've heard *other* people say, "We have three focus areas
this quarter: producing thirteenth-century Chinese pottery rep-
licas, incorporating subliminal images of Brad Pitt into the design
of our new commuter van, and optimizing our cows." Just for the

record, that isn't focus, it's all-inclusive mental smorgasbord and the reason your company is losing money so fast it'll make your head spin.

CHOOSE THE TYPE OF FOCUS YOU NEED

There are two ways to focus, and depending on the task, you'll have to decide which one is better for you. The first is content focus.

When you're in content focus, you load a project into your brain and do everything related to that project. If you're writing a report in content focus mode, you might spend the day writing, researching, calling people *strictly about the report topic*, brain-storming, and editing. Even though you're doing lots of different stuff, it's all so deeply related that your brain can stay with that project for the whole day.

Task focus is quite different. In task focus, you group together similar tasks, even if they don't involve the same project. For example, you may decide to spend the afternoon in the park with your cell phone and a notepad, returning every phone call on your to-do list, until you've finished all your calls utterly without distraction or interruption. Or you may group all your errands together into a single shopping trip, even though you're buying stationery supplies, Hello Kitty stickers, and that cheerleader outfit you've dreamed about since high school to wear for Halloween. While you're at it, you can drop by your therapist's office to work through any lingering issues you might have about reaching middle age.

Focus around single content areas when you need to keep an entire content area in mind and completeness and depth are what's important. Project management, writing, proposal writing, help-ing a client fix a problem, and completing a college application all would benefit from content focus.

Focus around the type of task when the tasks don't involve

keeping a lot of details in mind and it would take a long time to switch between types of tasks. Running to the post office, shopping, sorting stacks of incoming mail, and cooking several courses of a meal would all benefit from focus around task.

Some jobs require both task and content focus at the same time. If you have to respond to incoming customer requests immediately, *and* design a product, and you can't separate them on your schedule, you'll go crazy. Find out if you can redesign your job to separate your content focus tasks—like designing a product—from your task-focus interruptions—like responding to customer requests.

GROUP SIMILAR TASKS TOGETHER WHENEVER YOU CAN TO MAINTAIN FOCUS

Most of us have enough flexibility to shift our jobs around a bit. Moment by moment, we have the chance to group together similar tasks that require similar focus. Sometimes we don't even realize we're juggling multiple tasks. Start noticing where you think you're doing one thing but really doing several. My biggest gold mine was streamlining how I use word processing and presentation software.

When we write on computer, we write a sentence, read it, notice it could be better, start editing it, cut, paste, and revise the sentence six times before ever getting to the next one. If we forgot to turn off spell checking as mentioned in the conquering technology chapter, even our revisions are interrupted by little spurts of fixing typos. If our thoughts were flowing to begin with, they've now been treated to a five-minute diversion down Editing Lane. (I just rewrote this paragraph five times. 'Nuff said.)

We also do this with presentations. We spend 20 percent of our time writing the words, and 80 percent of the time customizing the sparkles, inserting animation, and "nudging" objects so they line up on the screen.

The problem is that we're mixing three very different tasks:

Creating a thoughtful piece of creative writing.

Editing and polishing our writing to make it flow.

Formatting your brilliance.

When you're going to write or create a presentation, just do that. Write. Keep moving forward. Yes, you'll have sentence fragments. You'll have misspellings, and you'll have somewhat fractured logic. That's nice. You'll fix it later.

When you keep moving, you let your mind follow your ideas all the way to the end. You get into a rhythm and can write pages and pages of content. Is it all good? Of course not. But that isn't the point, yet. The point is to get everything out. You'll clean it up later.

When you're done writing, put it away for a while. Then later, when you're in the mood to sink your teeth into something and wallow in self-criticism, get out your writing. Start at the top and go through, demolishing it. Cut, paste, rewrite. Shorten, lengthen, and wordsmith.

With your brain fully in edit mode, you don't need to think about what you still have left to say. It's all there. You can put your full attention on making your argument flow smoothly.

Tempted to start nudging those bullet points around on the screen? Spend all the time you need . . . *after* you're done editing.

Formatting is an utterly different task from writing. You can spend forever formatting, tweaking fonts, inserting colors, and including little animated bunny rabbits. Though presentation is important, it's only important if you have something worth presenting.

So make sure your content takes top priority. By separating formatting from writing, you keep from making work for yourself by switching back and forth between the two tasks. And there's another bonus—since you complete your text before you start formatting, if a deadline sneaks up on you, all that will suffer is the animated bunny you hoped would keep people from falling asleep, while your writing itself will be done and perfect.

When writing a report, you could choose to note the research you need for the many parts of your report. Then you could do all the research in one concentrated session, rather than switching back and forth between writing and researching.

DIVIDE YOUR LIFE INTO FOCUS, ADMIN, AND SPIRIT DAYS TO STAY FOCUSED

Completing one project—such as a presentation—requires different kinds of tasks, and so does life. As we saw above, we do our best work fastest when diving into one kind of task and building momentum and flow.

Usually the tasks that move us forward and help us get stuff done require focus. If you're a writer, writing is a task requiring focus, or a focus task. If you're a salesperson, prospecting and following up with clients are focus tasks. If you're a supergenius coyote with a hankering for desert fowl, creating elaborate Road Runner traps is a focus task.

Then there are other tasks that don't require so much focus, such as some types of paperwork. We have bills to pay, junk mail to toss, stuff to file, desks to neaten, phone calls to return. This is admin work. We don't necessarily love it, but our admin work builds the foundation for focus time. Admin time is often chockfull of nonfocus activities.

Finally, there's spirit time. That's when we do what nourishes our spirit. We spend time with friends and family. We draw, act, sing, play video games, and collect comic books—all the stuff that isn't about *doing*, but is about *being*.

When we try to mix focus, admin, and spirit stuff, we don't do any of them well. We spend our admin time thinking we should be working on focus tasks. We spend focus time wishing we had a chance to be feeding our spirit. And we spend spirit time feeling guilty that we aren't paying our bills. It keeps our therapist employed, but it's not so great for us. Feeling guilty is a lot of work, and it's not work that helps us do anything.

Skip the guilt and clean up this chaos by dividing your life into three different kinds of days: admin, focus, and spirit. Admin, focus, and spirit days have different kinds of content and different kinds of tasks. Admin days usually have lots of different content, but similar tasks (for example, filling out paperwork, filing, running errands). Focus days often involve strong content focus, such as deeply researching a problem and finding a solution. For some professions, focus days may have a strong task focus, as when a salesperson spends a focus day following up with prospecting calls. By separating out focus, admin, and spirit days, you'll get much better focus throughout the day.

Decide *in advance* what kind of day a given day will be. Then, only schedule tasks and appointments of that type for that day. You'll be able to get your brain into one mode and leave it there, so you get working faster. You also know that the other types of days are coming, so you skip all the worrying. When your brain knows tomorrow is a focus day, it will happily let you do admin tasks today without obsessing about how you're "supposed to be doing" focus stuff.

Once you've decided Monday is an admin day, you needn't do deep, focus tasks. You can file, sort, return phone calls, and do busywork to your heart's content. You know you're being productive because you know you're clearing out all the admin stuff that will free you up for a focus day, during which you'll get into the flow and finish your big presentation in a day instead of a whole week. Your animated bunny will approve!

On your focus Tuesday, you can turn off your phone, stop checking e-mail (unless that's part of your focus activities), and power ahead. You needn't think about admin tasks, because you know you'll have an entire admin day soon to catch up.

And on your spirit days, you can just "be." You know your admin tasks are getting handled. You know you're making progress on your focus tasks. Your spirit days become your time to indulge in just loving life. They once had a word for this, it was called a "weekend." Take heart: If you master the steps to work less and do more, you might someday experience a weekend as well!

When you start using this method, you may need several admin days to clear your mind and workspace enough for a focus day. This is normal. You're catching up and getting on top of your admin backlog. You'll have fewer spirit days at first, but soon your entire Saturday and Sunday will become available as your focus momentum ramps up. If you're lucky enough to be self-employed, you can keep adding spirit days. A self-employed colleague complains bitterly that he's stuck at just five spirit days a week. It seems any attempt to go to six hurts his near-seven-figure income. I nod sympathetically. Perhaps someone will write a Tony–award-winning tragedy about his plight.

Within a few weeks, you will notice you're on top of your admin tasks, and your admin days have an unusual amount of free time. The clue is when you find yourself watching *Harry Potter, the Unrated Director's Cut* in midafternoon.

When you start having those free blocks of time, convert an admin day into another focus day. And when you find you have many more focus days on your plate, turn one or two into a spirit day. The following table shows you how you might divide up your week.

MON	TUE	WED	THU	FRI	SAT	SUN
Admin Day	Focus Day	Focus Day	Admin Day	Focus Day	Spirit Day	Spirit Day

Stay Focused on Admin Days

Admin days by their very nature demand lots of running around, picking things up, and putting them down. You also have to get things out, like stamps and stationery, and put things away. This is all great fun, especially when you're three.

Part of the joy of admin days is that the tasks rarely require deep thought, so you can group otherwise unrelated tasks according to the materials you need. For example, you can address and mail bills, marketing material, and birthday cards all in one sitting. You just need to make sure the sitting includes a pen, paper, and postage.

And therein lies the way to get the most out of your admin days: Schedule groups of related admin tasks so you achieve Task Focus. Make all your phone calls at one time. Run all your errands at once. Group everything that happens at the same place. Block out times on your schedule so you know it will all get done. At ten a.m., you'll make calls and catch up on all things phone related. At one p.m., you'll spend an hour in the car, running errands.

Even though it's a day for random stuff, keep each group of activities pure so you can keep your brain groovin' along, getting more done (this is the "do more" part of "work less, do more"). If something happens that doesn't belong with your current task, delay it. A call comes in while you're sorting? Let it go to voicemail. Pick it up and respond during your phone-call period.

One important exception is Stuff You Do on Computer. We've already established that computers are evil, soul-sucking machines that exist to destroy your productivity, your life, and any remaining humanity that might exist in your workplace. If you sit down at one, the temptation will be to stay there all day.

Group similar computer tasks together, but at different times. Schedule e-mail time at 11 a.m., but printing your presentation handouts at two p.m. Otherwise, it's too easy for everything to glom together and become just "computer time." As anyone with a streaming video subscription knows, "computer time" is a dangerous thing.

Stay Focused on Focus Days

Even though focus days give you concentrated time for focus projects, you still have an attention issue. If you are working on multiple projects, your focus day itself may be full of switching from one project to another.

This keeps you firmly in driven-by-distraction mode. What's worse, if you aren't careful, you might get so engrossed in building a better mousetrap that you might totally lose track of that perpetual motion machine that's 80 percent done.

We separate focus, admin, and spirit days because each day requires a different style of thinking. Even on focus days, different projects require different thinking. Just when you have that beautiful mental image of the two-hundred-piece perfect mousetrap, you get distracted by an idea about perpetual motion. This may lead to a better mousetrap powered by perpetual motion, but mostly, it's just distracting.

Let's dedicate focus time for each project. Preassign time for each project on a focus day to ensure every project gets time to move forward.

Make a list of all your focus projects.

Schedule time for each in advance. Make sure each gets enough time to make progress.

If there's not enough time in your schedule to include all your focus projects, you're doing too much. Drop something!

A Sample Stever week

MON	TUE	WED	THU	FRI	SAT	SUN
Admin Day:	**Focus Day:**	**Focus Day:**	**Admin Day:**	**Focus Day:**	**Admin (1/2 Day):**	**Spirit Day**
(admin for all projects)	2 p.m.– 6 p.m. write + produce podcast	9 a.m. to noon write article *or* blog post	consulting biz send out invoices sort receipts	consulting biz	household stuff ——— **Spirit Day:** (rest of day)	

When you have multiple projects on your plate in one focus day, stay focused on one particular task by ignoring everything that doesn't have to do with the project you're working on *right now*. When you're working on your Ghoul-based Authoritarian Initiative, if you need to retrieve a related e-mail, scan your in-box paying attention *only* to the GAI-related e-mail. The Zombie-related messages get ignored *totally* for the next hour, until you switch to your dedicated block of Zombie time.

Schedule Slack Time

In addition to focus, admin, and spirit days, you need plain old slack time in order to get more done. Yes, that's right; if you have time set aside to do nothing, you'll end up getting more accomplished. That's because being able to juggle a dozen projects has a sinister downside. Let's say you have twenty projects humming along nicely. You are helping your mentee with their big presentation, filling out your yearly budget, and assembling the ant farm you plan to bring home to surprise your six-year-old.

While everything goes according to plan, this works. You're on top of the world, keeping the balls in the air, and life is humming along like a smoothly oiled machine.

Then, your mentee has an emergency schedule change and needs to meet you at four p.m. today. That was directly opposite your meeting with the folks in accounting to review your budget. They graciously agree to reschedule for the only remaining time slot before the budget deadline, eight a.m. tomorrow. Too bad you forgot that live ants are being dropped off directly at your desk with the 8:15 a.m. mail shipment. By nine the next morning, your desk is covered with ants, and the accounting department—none of them morning people—accidentally dropped a zero from next year's budget numbers. Oops.

One small crisis spills into your other commitments. The ripples spread until you have a dozen disasters on your hands because there was no space in your schedule for emergency cleanup, and no space in your mind to deal with the unexpected. As the ripples spread, each successive emergency demands more time to clean up and get back on track. Instead of working less, now *everything* is falling behind, which means everything will now take *more* work to get back on track and finished.

Stand up to the evil dominos and schedule time just to handle emergencies. For instance, block off half a day each week and label it "Slack." When one of your projects slips, use that time to start catching up. Your mind may resist. Since you never know in advance how you'll use the time, your mind will insist that you think of specific things to put in that time block. Don't do it! Slack time transcends the focus, admin, spirit distinction. Since you never know how it will be used, put it on any day where it fits, and use it to handle any kind of task that needs your love and attention.

The world will give you plenty of chances to use your slack time. If, by some slim chance, you have nothing to catch up on when that time block comes by, rest and relax. A huge disaster is probably right around the corner, and everyone will expect you to fix it, so now's a great time to catch up on your *X-Men* reading.

If you're tempted to schedule your slack time as if it were personal time, *don't.* Just because it appears to be open time doesn't mean it will be available for personal stuff when the time arrives. In fact, precisely the opposite. You're holding time in your schedule to catch up on all the obligations that would otherwise spill into your personal time, which will allow you to be at the office less. So that means your slack time is *in addition to* your personal time.

THE FOCUS CHALLENGE

All of which brings us to the focus challenge. This is when you get to stop lying to yourself and embrace the truth about how you work. Your feelings love multitasking. Your brain says your job *forces* you to multitask. The research disagrees, so I'm going to get personal. I *dare you* to try focusing for one week. Do it rigorously, the same way I tested how effective my technology was in the technology chapter.

Block your work week into admin and focus days (the spirit days are your treat for successfully completing the week). Schedule all your admin and focus work into the appropriate days. Group related tasks in admin days, and group related projects in focus days. Don't forget to schedule slack time. Then spend the week giving 100 percent attention to each task until you reach a natural breaking point. Keep a journal and jot down any objective measure of how much work you got done. It could be a number of people called, expense reports processed, papers filed, or romantic prospects e-mailed. Also jot down how you felt during the process—was it easier, more fun, et cetera. Note that if you're a chronic multitasker, you'll likely feel uncomfortable for the first few days as you crave your stimulation "fix."

At the end of a week, review your journal. If you got less done, at a lower-quality level, with less enjoyment, then go back to multitasking. I'll bet, however, that you do more with less work than you can even imagine. And if I'm wrong, I won't eat crow, but I *will* sacrifice and eat three slices of Oreo ice cream cake in a single sitting. It's only fair.

CHAPTER RECAP

- Eliminate distractions by deferring them to paper and then to designated interruption time.

- Set boundaries and say no.

- Stop multitasking; it doesn't work.

- Focus by grouping similar tasks or similar content. The choice depends on the matter at hand.

- Use focus days, action days, and spirit days to organize your week.

- Group related tasks into their own time block.

- Never mail-order ants.

STAY ORGANIZED

No matter how focused and streamlined you are with your time, if you spend your time rummaging around in files, boxes, and notebooks, looking frantically for the phone number of the psychic you're depending on to tell you how to get that promotion you've always wanted, then you're wasting time. If you're disorganized, you have to remember where everything is, and keep it all in your brain, which can be really painful if you're trying to follow the plot of your favorite reality TV show. Organized, you spend your work time doing productive stuff instead of searching for the tools you need to do the productive stuff. That's why staying organized is step 5 and an essential step on the journey to working less and doing more.

Many people confuse "organized" and "neat." I'm not a neat person. Nothing personal, neat people, but every time I see you, I mentally critique your wardrobe unfavorably because I'm so jealous I can't *be* you. It takes me a mere nineteen weeks to put everything away, and three hours later, my office looks like a cyclone blew through it. My brain doesn't do "neat."

Fortunately, my brain *does* do organized. Organized means a place for everything, and everything in its place—even things that don't have a place. The place may be in one of the several dozen piles of paper floating around the office, but as long as I always know *which* pile of paper, I can go straight to what I need, when I need it. In this step you'll learn how you, too, can get your brain to do organized.

Physical organizing is easy so we'll start with that. The trick is actually being able to get everything organized *quickly* when the piles start to pile up—we'll learn to do that. We'll also delve into some *mental* organizing tools that will allow you to get so much done you'll have to start making up excuses to your co-workers to explain your superhuman abilities. Tell them you acquired your powers after being bitten by a radioactive muskrat. For some reason, people don't ask for details. If they do, just bare your teeth and snort. In this chapter we'll cover everything from how to organize your file folders to how to organize your days and I'll tell you how to organize your physical space, multiple projects, multiple-step or multiple-person processes, time, and travel.

ORGANIZE YOUR PHYSICAL ENVIRONMENT

There's only one, simple principle to physical organizing: Make a place for everything. It can be a pile, it can be a shelf, it can be a drawer, it can be a spot under the bed, it can be a cabinet, or it can be a closet, though I strongly recommend that anything you keep in a closet come out eventually. I like to use piles. When first organizing, I often use sticky notes to label my piles. Write big and use brightly colored notes so they're pretty and attractive.

When you stumble over something that doesn't have a place, either throw it away or make a place for it. If you don't have any more room, then throw away something less important to make the space. Don't you *dare* rent a storage unit! They're a waste of time and money, and it seems like people are always discovering dead bodies the previous owners left in them, which causes all kinds of annoying legal complications and media attention.

File Effectively

Files make great places to put stuff, as long as the stuff is paper that fits in files. Files are the ultimate for clearing clutter. Just put something in a file, then into a cabinet, then close the door. Voila, you're done filing. But as with *any* organization system, you have to be able to find something once you've stashed it away. When you're doing the stashing, put things away by keeping in mind how you're going to find them later.

I learned this from my favorite childhood book, *From the Mixed-up Files of Mrs. Basil E. Frankweiler* by E. L. Konigsburg.

In it, a little girl, Claudia, must find a file proving whether Michelangelo created a beautiful angel statue in the New York Metropolitan Museum of Art. She's given one hour and a room with files from ceiling to floor. The catch: She doesn't know where the proof is filed. (My art-geek friends loved the book because the kids hide out in the Met. I loved it for the filing cabinets. I was destined to be an organization geek. So sue me.)

The first secret to good filing is choosing file names carefully. When you want those files, you'll have to remember the names.

For example, let's say you're an evil supergenius planning to take over the world (I might be projecting here, but bear with me). You create a plan to build a doomsday device and hold the world hostage. You have another plan to corner the market in thread (no more fashionable clothes, ever). And, of course, your fallback plan is creating Zombies to do your bidding. You might file all of them in one folder labeled "Taking Over the World." But that's way too general. Here's why: Imagine you're in the grocery store and you spot a canister of "Extra-Strength Zombie

Reanimation Powder." That pushes you to choose your Zombie plan. So, you come home, and start implementing your dastardly plan. But whenever you pull out your file, you have to leaf through notes on doomsday bombs and thread markets, all mixed up with Zombie files. What a mess!

The problem is your folder topic is too general. You need specific folders—one for each plan. A better labeling scheme would be three folders, one for each of your plans: *Doomsday Device, Thread Market Takeover,* and *Zombie Creation.* Then, when you grab a folder, you only get information on the project at hand.

Don't subdivide too far! If you divide your *Doomsday Device* folder into *Watch Dr. Strangelove for Ideas, Doomsday Device Thoughts,* and *Doomsday Device Materials Lists,* you've spread your material through so many folders you'll need to pull them all to get anything done. Be specific enough so you don't include irrelevant stuff, and general enough so each folder has everything you need on a topic.

Even when the stakes aren't quite as high as world domination, subdividing files makes a difference. When just getting started in business, I had a single file folder for my designer. Whenever we worked together, our back-and-forth paperwork went into that file. The file grew fatter than a hidden squirrel in a nut farm. I finally wrestled it into submission by having one file for billing and a separate file for each project, containing the creative briefs, schedules, and project plans for that project.

When you label a file, ask, "When will I likely need this?" Then ask, "What will I likely be thinking then?" Put the file there.

For example, I run workshops and do public speaking. I used to file sessions under my client's name. If the talk was "Oprah or Iacocca: Becoming a Powerful Leader" for Widgets, Inc., it would go under *Widgets, Inc.—Oprah or Iacocca.* While working for Widgets, Inc., that worked. I always found the file.

Years passed. Someone called and said, "I saw you do a session, 'Oprah or Iacocca,' once. Could you do it for my company?" Neither of us remembered where I'd given it. It wasn't under "O" for Oprah, or "L" for leadership. Oops! Where *should* I have filed it?

When am I likely to want that file? If Widgets, Inc., calls and says, "Please send us the handouts from that session." Or if someone calls and says, "Can you do your 'Oprah or Iacocca?' session?" Or if someone calls and says, "Do you have any leadership speeches?" And, I suppose, I'll also need it if someone asks, "What topics do you have already prepared?"

So far, I want to file the speech under "W" for "Widgets," "O" for "Oprah," "L" for "leadership," and "S" for "speech." But clients change titles to meet their needs, so filing it under "O" is a bad idea, since the title may change. Here's my solution: The speech folder gets labeled *Speech—Leadership—Oprah or Iacocca.* I put a sticky note in my *Widgets* file saying, "I did the leadership session Oprah or Iacocca for this client."

This puts all my speeches together in one part of my file drawer. I know I can find a speech by looking somewhere in the *Speech* area. Within that area, they're alphabetized by topic; here it's *Leadership.* Last, I still write the speech title on the label, just in case I need to find it by title.

If you file for retrieval like this, you'll find your files much easier to use. Let's review: File according to when you'll need the information and what you'll be thinking *at that time.* Make your file labels general enough to hold whatever you might want at that time, but specific enough that you're not leafing through lots of extra stuff. When you have files that could be filed in many different places, use a file label with a hierarchy of words, as I did with *Speech—Leadership—Oprah or Iacocca.* Use sticky notes to cross-reference the file from other files where it might be used.

Mrs. Basil E. Frankweiler does, indeed, have a file proving the origin of the Metropolitan Museum's statue. It's filed in a way that would make it easy for Claudia to retrieve, if only she thinks like Mrs. Frankweiler. Whether she manages the task . . . well, you'll just have to pick up the book and find out.

When in Doubt, Throw It Away

When you realize you *won't* be using something in the future, don't file or store it. Send it to landfill, instead. Your mind will scream bloody Heck. Our minds—a holdover from when we lived in trees and ate bananas—like to keep things. We're expert at inventing bogus excuses for why it's necessary. Let's blow those excuses out of the water *now*, so you can get on with cleaning.

"I'm afraid I'll need it someday." When you bought it, you thought you'd *need* a karaoke weed-wacker machine. "If I get rid of it then need it later," you think, "maybe I'll die!!" No, you won't. Label a file folder, *Stuff I threw out but might need to replace someday*. Photograph your beloved weed wacker, put the picture in the file, then sell it or throw it away. Your picture records the brand, model number, and what it looks like. In the unlikely event that your weeds someday need wacking, just bring your photo to the hardware store and they'll replace your machine lickity-split. You can even do this with books. I read a book, think it's wonderful, and get rid of it. But not before recording the book and author in *Books I may need again someday*. So far, I've repurchased only about three books.*

"But it has such sentimental value!" I am a sucker for sentiment. That pressed flower from fifth grade, given by my eleven-

---

* This book is an obvious exception. You need several *additional* copies, in fact, to send to friends. Buy them now. You'll like yourself better if you do, and I'll like you more, too.

year-old sweetheart, whose name I can't even remember? Surely I must keep it forever. . . . Not! Sentiment is just an excuse for memory. When you have Alzheimer's someday, you won't remember it anyway. Take a picture and punt the clutter.

Do keep really special things, but use limits. The doll your mother made you with her own hands? Keep it. The doll your mother bought you that simulates all natural body functions? Feed it to the earthworms. And when you find that unwashed garment, saved from your famous senior year prom after-party? Burn it, no matter how much the smell takes you back to better days.

Have a friend join you to help filter stuff that might be truly critical. You can't be trusted to make those decisions; you're too attached. Invite your friend Brian, who's visiting from his Buddhist monastery where he's studying with the Dalai Lama. After a decade of practice, he's unattached enough to be objective.

Consider tossing the following:

- Any pile you haven't looked at in a year. Have your friend scan the pile and pull out anything truly important. You'll be amazed at what you can find ("So *that's* where the IRS audit notice was! And all three reminder letters, too. Cool!")
- Your old books. Any book you haven't read in a few years goes to a library. That copy of *101 Uses for a Dead Cat* was hilarious when you were sixteen. It's time to move on.
- The boxes you meant to unpack when you moved in fifteen years ago. If you open them, sinister forces of nostalgia will give you excuses to keep them. Have them hauled away. Now.
- Anything under the bed that isn't capable of speech.

You'll find once you have reclaimed the space in your life, you'll feel liberated, you'll breathe better, and you just might remember what color your carpet is, after all.

Put Everything in Its Place More Quickly

Once you've tossed the things you don't need, there's still the little issue of putting everything else in its place. Since we're all about working less, let's be really, really lazy about this. Organize physical things quickly and easily by moving things where they should go immediately. If something would interrupt your physical organizing and take time to put away, you do it on paper. Your paper will end up with a personal map for the New World order in which everything is happily put away. Then you'll make reality conform to your master plan.*

To start putting things away and organizing quickly, make sure your trusty pad and pencil is nearby and just start grabbing items. Let's say you're cleaning your apartment before a party, or cleaning your office before your annual review. If an item's home is here in this room, put it away. Voila! It's cleaned up for real. But if you're in your office and you just grabbed that plate of half-eaten chocolate cake that lives on the floor under your desk, its home is in the kitchen sink or dishwasher (I hope). For now, set it neatly by the door. You've just started your pile of "things that belong in other rooms." Put all files-to-be-filed in one corner of your desk, then file them all at once. And yes, your secret stash of one thousand sticky pads that's outgrown its hiding place will go in the "things that belong back in the supply closet" pile.

Next time you leave for any reason, grab the items from that pile that belong where you're going. Take the items with you, and as soon as you arrive, put them where they belong. Once again, you've done real cleaning up. This will work for cleaning your

---

* The astute reader will note that this is actually a focus trick, disguised as a megalomaniacal exercise in political science. Organizing involves deciding where to put things and then putting them there. We're just separating out the two steps so we can make all our decisions at once and then do all the moving at once.

home up quickly, too. You're happily putting everything where it belongs . . . until you reach that invitation to the annual sales convention and masquerade you found buried under the centerfold from the current issue of *Earth Moving Farm Equipment and the Farmers Who Use It*. You know you want to go, but you needn't keep the brochure and so you don't want to file it or put it away; you just want to toss it. On your handy piece of paper, write the heading "Possible To-do Items." Jot down the information about the masquerade and throw away the invite. Do this for any object that generates a future to-do item—like that page of notes you just rediscovered and that you need to integrate into the memo you're writing. Write down the to-dos whether or not you know when you'll do them. Capture the action, throw or put away the item. Just keep moving. That's what I mean when I say you're doing things on paper; you're recording any potentially distracting actions you need to take and you only do them when they won't distract from your focus of organizing.

Sometimes you find immediate to-dos, like filling up your trash bag and discovering you have no more spares. You can't delay new trash bags. If you do, the current one grows legs and develops opinions of its own. You really don't want that to happen, so jot down the heading "Immediate To-dos" and write "grab new trash bags." Run out at your next break and do just those to-do items. Nothing goes in that category except buying new trash bags, taking out the existing trash, and bribing the janitor to walk off with the poster of babies dressed as jazz players your office mate hung on the wall over your ficus tree.

I've saved the scariest for last: stuff without a home that you don't know what to do with. Some things don't have a home and have no action implications, but you still want to keep them. For example, the Queen Elizabeth sculpture a client gave you as an appreciation gift. It's made entirely out of macaroni and glitter. You put it on your desk right next to that invitation to your best friend's latest wedding. The sculpture is obviously worth keeping, but where does it go? The dust bunnies solemnly look on as you spend five minutes choosing its resting place. You just put the brakes on your cleaning, as that decision knocked you right into low gear.

When something has no home, but you still need to clean it up quickly, just stash it anywhere. But add a new category to your tracking sheet called "Swept under rug." Note the item and where you stashed it. After you're done cleaning up, go through this list and find real homes for these objects. If several things all need the same kind of home, create a system to deal with them so next time clean-up will be easier. I noticed half of my "under rug swept" category was Alanis Morrisette CDs. One CD-rack purchase later, the problem is fixed for good. What you've done is turned the tough part of clean-up—making decisions and finding homes for all your homeless items—into a cheerful list just by writing it down instead of actually doing anything about it. That comes later, and *now* is the time to decide when later will be.

The moment you add something to your "Swept under rug" list, schedule an appointment with yourself to go through and deal with all that crap. Put it on your calendar for your next admin day, and use every motivational accountability trick in the book (this book, at least) to make sure you deal with every item on that list.

When the time comes to lift your rug and negotiate with what you find, it's not much of a negotiation. Grab your "Swept under rug" list and cross out the words "Swept under rug." Write in, "Stuff to throw away." Congratulations! You just committed to getting rid of all that pesky stuff. You have fifteen minutes to scan the list, decide what you'll rescue, and what you'll do with it. You can find a home for it, *now*, or give it away. Sometimes you can't find a home right now because you need accessories. Perhaps you need to buy a new bookshelf, or a filing cabinet, or a shock-proof cage. If so, *immediately* schedule the trip on your calendar. If you're not willing to schedule the appointment, that's a sign you can just toss the whatever-it-is straight into landfill.

Did you catch that life-changing principle as it zipped by? Most of the time, we look at stuff and decide what to throw away. We do it when cleaning. We do it when processing our e-mail inbox. We do it when processing incoming paper. "Can I afford to get rid of this peacock feather encrusted fountain pen? Maybe not. I may need it someday." Since your brain thinks of the things as already part of your life, it doesn't want to give them up.*

Instead, tell your brain that you've already thrown everything away. Then invite your brain to rescue just the things to keep. To your brain, "rescuing" sounds like a lot of work. "Rescue? As in, dive into freezing water and drag someone to safety during a hurricane? I don't think so! Hand me the bonbons and toss me the remote control. I'm in for the night." You'll find that suddenly far fewer items need to be saved. This tip is so good I'll repeat it: Don't save everything and toss what you want to get rid of; get rid of everything and rescue what you want to save!

When You Have a Really Big Organizing Job

If you have a really big organizing job, and don't have time to finish it, you need a new organizing strategy so that you don't end up with half-sorted, piles-waiting-to-go-elsewhere neatness mixed with glorious preorganized chaos. Instead, use focus and completely separate the sorting task from the moving task. Tackle the sorting plan first.

You don't know what you'll find, so you can't plan for this . . .

---

* I'm making this sound more Disney than it is. This is a principle from behavioral decision theory called "anchoring to the current state of affairs." I'm just making it more fun to read about.

whatever it is . . . completely in advance, but you *can* decide for general categories. Then when you find something, the decision is made. You just grab it and go.

Let's say you need to organize your room but have a very important appointment in forty-five minutes and your room is no match for forty-five minutes. You see socks. They peek out of your briefcase. They flirt with you from the floor, bureau, and lampshade. Socks. Not even pairs of socks, just socks. "Socks" looks like a good category. You can decide up front that socks go into a big pile in the middle of the room. After you've completed the whole job of organizing the room, you can pair, wash, and put away the socks. You've decided the sorting plan in advance, so when you find a sock you know where it goes—the pile. And you know what to do with the pile when you're done.

Plus, there's change everywhere. Decide in advance to use a plastic box as its home. Change goes right into the Tupperware. Later, you'll visit the giant Change Sorting Machine at the grocery store. You'll give them $2,000 worth of pennies, in return for $1,800 worth of cash. A bargain, at any price.

Maybe you're besieged by receipts. Only two kinds matter: tax-deductible ones or receipts you can expense, and receipts for returning products. Prepare two envelopes ahead of time, "tax-deductible receipts" and "might-want-to-return." Any receipt you find goes straight into the envelope where it belongs. Any that don't fit, you'll plan to send to the landfill.

These are my categories. Your categories may differ. Maybe you have vintage handbag collections, and must decide whether the rhinestone encrusted Sushi lunchbox is part of your collection, or just an unfortunate consequence of a three-martini lunch. Deciding in advance will streamline your organizing so if you need to call it quits only thirty minutes into a two-hour organizing spree, you'll know where everything goes so you can easily restart and complete the task when you have the time. You save time by making decisions only once, instead of with each item. Plus once the decisions are made, you can fit in the actual doing as time allows—which lets you fit it into blocks of time here and there that would otherwise go wasted.

Before you start actually organizing, wander through the room with your trusty pad of paper. Instead of noting specific items, jot down *categories* of things that can all be dealt with the same way. If you see something that doesn't fall into a category on your sheet, think for a few minutes and identify the category it belongs to. You'll end up with a list like this:

OFFICE CLEANING	
Categories	**Sample items**
Files	Saved receipt folder, folder with vendor contract.
Meeting notes	About two dozen different sheets of paper throughout the office. Notes about a grant to apply for.
Memos to read	Strategic planning summary, Ghoul Authoritarian Initiative alert, revisions to the budget.
Articles I've read	*How to Get Rich Without Using a Single File Folder (hated it).*
Articles to read	Saras Sarasvathy articles on entrepreneurship. Len Schlesinger articles on running a service firm.

APARTMENT CLEANING	
Categories	**Sample items**
Game controllers	Bundle of cords with occasional buttons, joystick, Wii controllers, guitar controller, drum controller, golf club, tennis racket.
Comic books	The pile of *Green Lantern* issues by the door. My *X-Men Phoenix* series, a stack of miscellaneous Anime, my complete *Elfquest* collection, a Doonesbury compilation, and my complete collection of Barefootz.
Dirty clothes	Those socks. Yes, those. And that … er, T-shirt. I think— well, whatever that furry thing with armholes is.
Books I've read	They're everywhere: *The Halo Factor, Succubus in the City* (*love* Nina Harper), *Outliers,* and *Using Your Brain—For a Change.*
Tasty food	Package of Twinkies by the bedside. Marshmallow peeps from Easter (they never go bad, do they?), raw pasta for snacking purposes.

Before you touch a single thing, decide what you'll do with each category. Write it down so you don't cheat and make exceptions for things that don't deserve exceptions.

CATEGORY	WHAT I'LL DO WITH THEM
Files	Stack in "to file" pile. File today between 4 p.m. and 5 p.m.
Meeting notes	Using papier-mâché, form them into a likeness of the meeting facilitator, stick pins in each, then burn them.
Memos to read	Throw away any over six months old. Read the rest between 1 p.m. and 4 p.m. next Wednesday.
Tasty food	Wrinkle my nose and sniff. If it smells bad, throw it away. Otherwise, put it in "for kitchen" pile and then put all "for kitchen" items away today at 5 p.m. If any of the food wrinkles its nose back, throw it out no matter how it smells.

Then kick yourself into action and do it. I use paper organizing for e-mail, paper mail, sorting out books, dismantling piles that have outlived their usefulness (yes, I know which pile a given item is in, but that doesn't mean I know everything in a given pile), straightening up a car, storing camping equipment, and matching up jobs and how they fit my many Zombie warriors. The simple trick of deferring the hard decisions to paper gives you the focus to organize in a snap. The organizing is easier, and all that time you used to spend trying to find stuff can now be spent doing something more deeply meaningful, like joining a wine-tasting club, or a scotch-tasting club, or a scotch-tape-testing club.

HOW TO QUICKLY ORGANIZE A MESS
IN THE MIDST OF A PROJECT

As much as my ego doesn't want to admit it, there will come a time where you won't have followed my stellar advice on organizing and so you will find yourself trying to complete several urgent projects while sitting in the middle of a monumental mess created from the paperwork, books, folders, e-mail, snail mail, phone messages, and other items related to each project. Because said project needs to be completed tomorrow, you simply don't have time to take my advice and do a thorough organizing job. But you can't possibly get any work done when everything is so disorganized. The secret organizing weapon is simple: Filter.

Going through item by item and deciding what to do with it would take forever, and would burn up most of your mental energy. Fortunately, there's a better way to grab just what you need. It relies on your brain's little-known but very powerful superpower, filtering. You can filter things much more easily than you can triage and categorize. Filtering keeps your brain focused in one place even when you're bombarded with chaos. It's easy to use filtering to save the day!

Pile everything incoming in one big pile. Think of your first project, scan the pile, and pull out everything related to that project. For example, set your mental gears to the Feed Yelena's Pet Boa While She's on Vacation project. In moments, you can spot everything related to that project—a phone message from the vet, an e-mail reminding you of the feeding schedule, and a live white mouse to feed to the snake. (The mouse is easy to spot. Its box has a picture of a young girl holding the mouse gently, with the caption "Somebody loves me" on the side. How sweet!) Leave everything else in a pile and just filter out what you need when you need it.

ORGANIZE YOUR BRAIN

You've taken another step toward a future of working less by organizing your office and house. Now they're nice, neat, and organized and you won't waste time looking for the right pen—you'll know exactly where it is, since you've categorized them by color, tip size, ink type, and barrel width (am I projecting, here?). But you don't get off that easily. These things won't stay organized unless you organize your brain to keep them that way. The biggest organizing task happens where no one else can see it: in your brain. You think your workspace was chaotic? Just be thankful we humans can't see how disorganized our own thinking is. It makes a messy office look pristine by comparison.

I, sadly, was playing with my super X-ray specs attempting to solve all twenty-four sides of a Rubik's HyperCube at once when I glanced in the mirror. Several hundred hours of therapy later and I realize that my brain isn't suitable for keeping track of much of anything.

Someday when I can afford an entourage, I'll have a perky assistant named Okra who will keep track of everything for me. Until then, I use crutches to manage the complexities of twentieth-century life. My favorite crutch is engineer's graph paper.* It's a general-purpose tool that can help you manage *anything*! I've seen it used to track projects, to monitor the progress of different teams during a scavenger hunt, to organize a three-day, two-hundred-character interactive theater event, to keep

---

* And the Pilot G2-05 mechanical pencil, the Pentel Shaker pencil, and the Pilot G-02 0.38 blue retractable gel ink pen. And before you say anything, I am *not* obsessive about my stationery supplies! Obsessive would be if I knew the model numbers by heart, instead of simply keeping all of them in my pocket at all times so I can just grab one and write the model number down right from the barrel.

track of a year's worth of programs at a yoga institute, and to make sure that *all* of the octuplets are getting fed and changed properly.

Use Graph Paper to Stay Organized

Want to know exactly how graph paper can transform your life and make you more organized? Let me explain how I use it. I'm the point person for four student projects. I have to keep track of four projects comprised of 22 students, 3 faculty members, and 4 sponsors, who only have to deal with 16 or 17 administrators around 3 different topics? What could be easier?

Herding cats. That could be easier. I'm easily confused. I could keep track of Mommy and Daddy when I was young because one of them had a beard. I wasn't always sure which, but at least I could tell them apart.

My project started out easy. I wrote up the project description for one group and sent it to them. Then I began the project description for group two, but the faculty member for group three called to chat. So we outlined group three's project, while I accidentally sent the group two description to the administrator for group one.

Then I had to get back to project two—or was it one—to help them schedule their next meeting with the administrators. Er, which administrators? I think the administrator I was just talking to was from project two. Or one. Or three. Or . . . argh!

What made this so hard to deal with is that the projects were similar. They all had students, faculty advisers, sponsors, and administrators. Plus, I had to do the same things for each project: Create a project overview, prep the administrators who would be talking with the students, and check in with the faculty sponsor to set up a schedule.

Because the projects were so similar, I got confused about what I'd done on which projects. Salvation came in the form of my trusty engineering graph paper. That's graph paper with a wide column one, and the rest of the columns narrow.

On each row, I wrote the names of the student team. To protect the innocent, let's call them Cougar, Buffalo, and Snort.

I labeled each column with the steps the team had to go through: project overview written, admins prepped, faculty check-in complete. There were lots of other steps, but you get the idea.

As each step got completed for each team, I would just check it off in the grid at the intersection of the team name and the step. When Snort's faculty adviser interrupted the phone call with Cougar where we were planning the project overview, I was able to check off the Snort/Faculty-Check-in-Complete box, so I wouldn't forget and recheck-in later. Then when I finished with Team Cougar's overview, I could check that off. With a single glance, I now know which teams still need to do which phases.

Sometimes you need to track information on a project-by-project basis. In that case, I merge a few columns together and write the information right on the tracking sheet. Since each team has a different weekly check-in time, I create a column called "Check-in Time" and just write in each team's check-in time on their line.

My grids often go onto the cool engineering graph paper I mentioned before. But if you're so glued to your computer that you use sunscreen to prevent your pasty white skin from getting burned by the monitor's glare, you can do this easily in a spreadsheet or word-processing document. Just do me a favor, please, and don't waste too much time resizing your columns. Your computer is a tool, not your silicon master.

The grid technique isn't just limited to projects. You can use it anytime you have the same set of steps you'll be doing with many different people.

If you're on a campaign to get the people in your office to approve of you and reinforce your feelings of worth as a human being, you might as well be organized about it. Your rows would be the names of each coworker. The columns would be the steps in your relationship-building plan: Meet with each one, uncover mutual interests, recommend a thoughtful book, learn their middle name, swap stories of your traumatic childhood, and then have a nice conference with them and an HR representative, where the three of you discuss boundary issues.

SAMPLE PROJECT TRACKING GRID					
	write overview	faculty check-in	team colors chosen	war cry selected	check-in time
Cougar	X		X		Monday, 3 p.m.
Buffalo	X		X		Wednesday, 8 a.m.
Snort		X		X	Saturday, 2 a.m.

Sample Grid to Track Renting an Apartment

A group of tenants could use this grid to keep track of what they need to apply for an apartment. Checked boxes in the first column apply to the entire group, while other checked boxes apply to individuals.

MULTI-ROOMMATE CHECKLIST	Alan	Blake	Sasha	Eric	Alicia	Steve	Date
Application submitted	✓	✓	✓	✓	✓	✓	
Co-signer application submitted	✓	✓	✓	✓	✓	✓	
Lease signing							
Lease signed	✓	✓	✓	✓	✓	✓	
Co-signer signed lease	✓	✓	✓	✓	✓	✓	
Lead law initialed	✓	✓	✓	✓	✓	✓	
1st month's rent sent	✓						
Signed lease scanned into computer	✓						
Security deposit-related							
W9 filled out and submitted for security deposit	✓						
Security deposit sent	✓						
Security deposit account # received	✓	Account #					
On-site issues							
All furniture arranged to be delivered	✓						
All roommates have their set of keys	✓	✓	✓	✓	✓	✓	
Mailbox labeled with our names	✓						
Parking passes obtained	✓	✓	✓	✓	✓	✓	

Use Forms to Organize Your Information

Sometimes you need to organize more information than a mere checked box can handle. Information needs a home, too. Your brain can only hold five to nine chunks of information at once, so your brain is *not* a good place to store lots of detailed stuff. When you're collecting information about something with many moving parts, create forms you can use to organize the information.

A good form has a space for all the information you'll need to fulfill the form's purpose. It acts as a checklist—any blank areas are a reminder that there's information you still have to obtain—and it's a record of the information you've managed to dig up. It's also a learning tool. As you use a form, if you discover it's missing critical information, you add fill-in areas to the form and next time, your form does the work of remembering what you need.

The best forms are the ones you design yourself, since they meet your needs perfectly. When traveling to do public speaking, for example, I would often visit a city for just a few hours. The first time, I gleefully hopped on the plane and arrived in Hoboken . . . only to realize I had no idea whether my host was picking me up at the airport, whether I was supposed to rent a car, or even whether I was supposed to go to a prespeech dinner or simply show up right before the speech.

The keys to creating a good form:

- Create space for all the information you think you'll need.
- Leave some blank space for free-form notes for notes you hadn't anticipated. Later, you can add spaces on the form for information you add.
- Label each space so you know what goes there. (I know this sounds obvious. Humor me. I used to jot down phone numbers with my travel arrangements with no label. Is it my host? The rental car company? The hotel? Having labeled spaces for each of those saved the day!)

My assistant and I gradually designed a form that let me put everything I needed on one page:

Traveling to destination	Airline, flight#, departure date & time	Arrival time, terminal
	(transfer flight if applicable)	Arrival time (if applicable)
If being met, who will meet me?	Person, emergency contact phone#	
If driving myself	Rental car company, reservation#, phone#	
Immediate destination upon arrival?		
Hotel	Address, phone#, reservation#, type of room	Check-out date & time
Pre-speech event (e.g. consulting or facilitation engagement, mixer, etc.)	Date/time	Location
Speech	Date/time	Location
	Contact person on day of speech, phone#	
Return home	Airline, flight#, departure date & time	Arrival time, terminal
	(transfer flight if applicable)	Arrival time (if applicable)

Forms make the most sense when organizing information you'll use over and over. You'll create forms to keep track of individual Zombies in your World Domination Army, because you want to track the same information about each of your many thousand Zombie soldiers. For one-time events, such as cornering the world fashion market, you may find it useful to create a form or two, but there's no need to be so structured about it. Once you have a stranglehold on the fashion industry, you won't need to stage a second takeover. Just declare anyone who opposes you as hopelessly out of style, and you win. If you'd like to borrow my tie-dyed T-shirts for your campaign, just ask.

Use File Folders to Track Physical Objects Through Their Lives

Your forms can help you sort information, but what about the physical stuff that comes with all those to-dos? We discussed file folders earlier as holders for stuff we want to archive and retrieve later. In-work paperwork doesn't belong in reference files, however, since it's just passing through. You can use file folders in a different way to organize ongoing-process paperwork. By process paperwork, I mean the paperwork that keeps stuff moving. Like the tenants above, who are juggling a dozen types of paperwork, you need a way to keep them all straight. Many jobs involve managing lots of paperwork. Pretend you're a high school teacher who gets 125 papers in one day—twenty-five papers from five different classes. File folders are a fine tool for taming process paperwork, too. Just watch.

You do stuff to all those papers. Maybe you read them, grade them, write comments, or feed them to your dog (it's about time *teachers* should be able to use the excuse, "My dog ate your paper"). When you want a paper, you'll be asking one of a few questions: "Where are the ungraded papers to grade?" "Where are the finished papers to hand back?" and "Where are the papers I need to review again?"

These questions form a road map for the process each paper goes through. You collect it, then you grade it, then you hand it back. Some papers may need to be reviewed again, so you rereview them before handing them back.

Here's the solution: Grab three file folders. Label them *Grade, Hand back,* and *Review.* When you collect papers, put them all in the "Grade" folder. After grading a paper, put it in the *Hand back* folder or, if you find you need to review it later, in the *Review* folder.

Now at any moment, you know exactly what's going on with each paper, since it's always in a folder that tells you what to do with it. When you're in the mood to work, just grab the *Grade* or *Review* folder and get to work.

Once those folders are empty, your *Hand back* folder will be full and ready to hand back to the students. Since you have three classes whose papers you grade, you might want three sets of folders, one for each class.

You can track your clients and prospects using folders, too. Set up five folders: *Prospects, Dropped Prospects, Negotiation, Active Clients,* and *Ex-Clients.* When someone calls or gives you their card, put their contact info and why they're calling in the *Prospect* folder. Use a full sheet of paper and staple their business card to it. When you start discussing terms, move it to the *Negotiation* folder. If they bail, toss 'em into *Dropped Prospects* and check back occasionally in case their needs change. Otherwise, they go into *Active Clients.* You can scan that folder to get your client list. When your engagement is over, their paper goes into *Ex-Clients.* In an ideal world, you send your ex-clients a tasteful holiday card and a bouquet of flowers on their birthday. Dream on.

You can use this system to track *any* process. For example, in organizing our all-important Zombie world domination project, every Zombie recruit has to go through several steps. First, the Zombie has to be identified, then sprinkled with Zombie reanimation powder. Once reanimated, the Zombie needs to be outfitted with a mind-control ray, issued a uniform, and sent out to do your bidding.

Each of those steps is a file folder. The first folder, *Recruits Identified,* has an information sheet on every zombie. The second folder is *Recruits Reanimated.* Once a recruit has been sprinkled with powder, their information sheet gets moved from the *Identified* to the *Reanimated* folder. The *Reanimated* folder now has a sheet for all the Zombies who need mind-control rays and uniforms. Once those are issued, you move the information sheet into a folder labeled *Active Zombie Army.* And of course, you have a final folder, "Reclaim for spare parts," so when an active Zombie soldier finally dissolves into goo on the battlefield, you can take appropriate salvage action.

(Who knew building a Zombie army would be so complicated? Or that using folders correctly could make it so easy?)

When my process is complicated, I use the folders to remember the details. On the inside of the folder, I write a reminder of the next steps for papers in that folder. So inside the *Reanimated* folder, I, er, I mean, *someone,* would write: Issue ray gun and move to *Active Zombie Army* folder.

Next time you have a complicated process, make it easy by breaking it down into steps and creating a file folder for each step. And if you're a teacher with troublesome students, just toss their papers into the folder labeled *Feed to Dog* and at long last, you'll be able to use that excuse, yourself.

Steps in a process	Once step is done, transfer to folder	What to do with items in that folder (tape to inside of folder)
Identify Zombies.	Identified	Sprinkle with reanimation powder.
Reanimate Zombies.	Reanimated	Requisition uniforms, mind control rays, etc.
Zombie outfitted with gear.	Active Zombie army	Zombie takes over world on my behalf, while I sip fruit-flavored beverages on secluded island.
Zombie melts into goo.	Reclaim for spare parts.	Send out salvage team.

ORGANIZE YOUR DAYS

Not only is assembling a Zombie army a huge process, but your body, itself, goes through a daily process. Once it's a finely tuned instrument, you can get the most done the fastest by organizing your work around what comes easily, *when* it comes easily. So now let's talk about how to organize your days to help you get the most done in the shortest amount of time.

We have natural rhythms. Some times of day, it is easier to do intense thought work. Sometimes, you're more sociable and outgoing. Still other times, you're not good for much except napping.

We all know about "morning people" and "night people." I am a night person; I have a promising career as a rock musician, someday. We night people *have* to work late. That's when the world gets quiet so we can think. There are also morning people. *Shudder.* One boss was *gasp* a morning person. He held staff meetings Monday at eight a.m. The morning people were there, chipper, smiling, and as energetic as ever. We hate them.

The rest of us were wasted. We could barely open our eyes. He thought we'd contribute. What a joker! He couldn't have done a better job of making sure he caught us at our physical, emotional, and mental bottom. It was work just to keep our eyes open, and we were getting nothing done. Although, we did dream. We dreamed about meeting him in a dark alley, at night, when *we're* awake, and *he's* asleep.

We have an emotional cycle, a physical cycle, and a mental cycle. All three need recharging. Pace your work to recharge all three and you'll get more rest and more done than trying to push straight through.

We drain our physical cycles with stress, and we recharge with sleep and exercise. We need to get enough sleep, and it has to be quality sleep. We also need exercise. And no, typing doesn't count. So next time you go to the convenience store to buy candy, walk instead of drive. It's a start.

Our emotional cycles recharge with positive emotion: feelings of gratitude and connection to life meaning. We spend our day lurching from emotion to emotion, reacting to the world around us. Take time out. Reconnect your life meaning. Feel grateful. If nothing else, imagine butterflies. Butterflies always make me smile.

Mental recharge happens in downtime: sleep and daydreams. That's why the best ideas happen in the shower. No, it's not those toxic shower mold fumes after all. It's because your brain is built to think when you're doing something else.

Look at your daily schedule. Rate your appointments and to-do items as physical, emotional, or mental. Notice if each uses or restores energy. Use a − if the activity uses energy, a 0 if it's neutral, or a + if it gives you energy. For example, supervising teenagers might be a mental rest but a physical and emotional drain.

Now look at the time of day. Is each activity scheduled when it best fits your rhythm?

Revise your schedule so you match what you do with the best time to do it. Maybe shifting your phone calls from afternoon to morning works better. Or working out at three p.m. makes more sense, since it's when you need to replenish mentally and emotionally. Customize your schedule around your rhythms to keep your energy smooth and flowing all day long. That way, you'll be at your peak for each kind of task. You'll get it done faster and you'll do a much better job.

APPOINTMENT	Physical	Emotional	Mental	Time
Writing book	0	0	—	10 a.m.–1 p.m.
Working out	+	0	+ (if I listen to music)	3 p.m.
Meeting with boss	—	—	0	11 a.m.
Hug my Sweetie	+	+	— (we talk a lot)	6 p.m.

When you're organized, you simply eliminate all the work involved with finding and arranging stuff. You know where everything is and where it goes, whether it's your office you're dealing with, or your current projects, your body's daily ups and downs, or the paperwork for your Zombie army recruits. You can organize using graph paper, grids, and by using paper to capture the organizing that would take too long to do physically. All the time you used to spend hunting through drawers or little scraps of paper are gone. Now that you're organized, you're working less; all you're doing is work that actually moves you toward your goals. In the next few chapters, we'll explore how to do more by optimizing, enlisting others, and using leverage so you'll be working even smarter.

CHAPTER RECAP

- The key to physical organizing is having a place for everything and everything in its place. If something doesn't have a place either throw it away or make a place for it.

- File stuff away according to how you plan to retrieve it.

- For faster physical organizing, organize on paper and then move all the physical stuff at once.

- Organize your brain and the information you need with graph paper, grids, and forms

- Organize your days according to your natural rhythms and cycles.

STEP 6

STOP WASTING TIME

At this point, you know your purpose, you've turned off your oh-so-important social media and PDAs, you've eliminated outside distractions, and you're focused so you can actually get some work done. What else could go wrong?

Well, if you're like me, you can lock yourself alone in a room with nothing but the work you need to do, you can work your butt off but still find you're working more and not doing more. The problem is that even with utter focus, you can still waste time, and that's where step 6 comes in.

Time wasting comes in a few convenient varieties. You can do stuff you think is work but actually isn't; you can work on stuff that doesn't give you the biggest bang for your buck; you can get caught up in doing way more than you need; you can make decisions that take ten times as long as they need to; and you can get stalled by very basic, simple stuff that gets in your way that you never clean up.

In this chapter, we're going to blast through all of those time wasters. Once you're ready to go, you'll be able to get more done and make more progress, with much less work.

MAKE SURE WHAT YOU'RE DOING IS WORK

Sometimes, what we call work, is work today, but won't be to-morrow. Work changes over time. Today's work is tomorrow's waste of time. When Warren Buffett started out in the 1950s, a ten-thousand-dollar investment decision was a big deal for him. Now that he makes Richie Rich look like a pauper, any decision involving less than hundreds of millions (if not billions) of dollars is not the best use of his time. He'd better not think of a ten-thousand-dollar investment as work. In his mind, that should fall under the heading of frivolity.

Work is whatever you're doing that most meets your goals *as they are today.* In your first job, mindlessly checking off forms and filing them in slot A or B may be a big part of work. Once you get noticed by the president in charge of vice, however, you get promoted to manager. At that point, someone *else* better be checking the forms! Your most workish time should be spent clarifying the goals of your group, aligning the work with the larger goals of the company, and making sure your direct reports are motivated and have what they need to do their jobs. What your previous job called "that weird fluff that managers do all day," your new job calls work. If your work shifts but you don't, you'll spend your time in the double-checking of forms, rather than in the clarifying, talking, and herding of the catlike humans who report to you that should make up the bulk of your workday. Then if you want to finish your work, you'll have to sacrifice your personal time.

Your old work still needs to be done, though. It's just that *you* need to unlearn it. Before you unlearn it, teach someone else and delegate it. Then their today work is your yesterday work, and you can focus on today's today work so tomorrow you'll be doing tomorrow's today work, and your tomorrow will be spent doing what will then be yesterday's today work. It's simple!

When you get any new job, you *always* have to redefine what work means to you. Whatever was work in your old job may not be anymore unless it's part of your new job. If the old work isn't getting done and you want to do something about it, the best you can do is find someone to take it over.

USE THE 80/20 RULE TO STOP WASTING TIME

Just doing today's work isn't enough. That will keep you working and doing, but working *less* means picking and choosing the work that's most important to your goals. Bernice is in charge of putting together our annual management meeting. With her keen eye for design and her charming way with people—charm that only improves when she uses mouthwash regularly—she's a natural at event planning. Unfortunately, she really *loves* flower arranging, and she isn't so keen on arranging all those complicated plane flights for the speakers. Flower arranging is, indeed, part of the work that needs to be done. But getting speakers is more important. Don't be a Bernice! Put your efforts behind what's most important using the 80/20 rule.

To illustrate why the 80/20 rule is important let's take a look at the success of the Home Shopping Network. It's not the average customer like me that keeps that business profitable. I just buy a faux diamond-studded hairpiece once every couple of years. Their profit comes from the tiny group that buys *hundreds* of items every week. If they want to sell product, the network should stop thinking about me and my hairpiece (hard to do, I know) and spend their time figuring out how to sell another doggie comforter to dear Bernice, who already has seventeen of them, in a wide variety of colors.

That principle has a name. It's called the 80/20 rule or the

Pareto principle. It means that most of what happens comes from a small number of causes. A few customers account for most of your profit. Your top employees produce as much as most of the rest put together. And most likely, your meaning and happiness in life comes from a tiny part of how you spend your time.

This is good news! It means when you look over your Life Map (or even just your current work goals), most of your progress will come from just a few actions. If you can identify those most-important actions, simply do more of those and less of the busy-work and you'll be home free. For you math geeks out there, think about it this way: let's say 20 percent of your activities give you 80 percent of your results. If you double the amount of time you spend on those Most Excellent activities and stop doing anything else, you'll only be working 40 percent of your time and getting 160 percent of the results you used to get. *That* is working less and doing more! Identifying your own Trusty 20 Percent depends on your job.

You can figure out your most important 20 percent by logging how you spend your time, analyzing all your activities, drawing graphs, and doing lots of stuff that would impress your ninth-grade teacher. Give it a rest. I'm willing to bet with five minutes' thought, you could list your key activities. Fill in this table:

What current tasks are your most important use of time?	What do you not do *now*, that would produce great results if you did?	What do you do now that *seems* to be work, but doesn't get spectacular results?
Finishing pending proposals, such as the proposal for client X.	Regularly called client X to find out what her current needs are.	Spend a half hour each day replying to nonessential email.
Preparing the marketing plan for the product launch.	Reach out to members of the PR committee so they're on my side when I pull the cute weather balloon stunt.	Copyediting the one paragraph blurb on the box.

Now, do more of columns one and two, and less of column three. Yes, it *is* that easy to stop wasting time!

DON'T WASTE TIME ON PERFECTIONISM

Being a brainiac, myself, I have even managed to find ways to waste time when I'm doing nothing but my Trusty 20. My crowning time waster is perfectionism. They say the perfect is the enemy of the good. My boss once said, "You spend most of your time getting your work quality from 80 percent to 98 percent, when everyone would be happy with 70 percent." I understand what he meant, but I just can't help it. I'm weak; I love perfection. I attended a Zombie march. Two hundred people dressed as Zombies, shambling along the city streets, boarding buses, grunting at the windows of restaurants, and generally doing what Zombies do.

I wanted a *perfect* costume! That meant makeup. And tailored rotten clothes. Maybe even raiding a graveyard, to find clothes taken from a real corpse. It turns out that raiding graveyards is illegal (who knew?), so I found myself stymied, not to mention running out of time.

Then I remembered "good enough." This is a Zombie march, for goodness' sake. "Good enough" was a few spoiled vegetables, torn jeans, tomato sauce, and green slime. For green slime, I settled on green face masque, to moisturize my skin, even as I pretended it was rotting off. (Talk about killing two birds with one stone, but moisturizing one of the birds.)

It became fun to fantasize about how low I could push "good enough." Would it be okay to attend as a two-day-old Zombie who hadn't started decomposing yet? Maybe I could just buy a rubber mask of a politician. People would instantly assume I was some sort of evil being from Heck.

Perfectionism affects more than just Zombie marches. I've seen people spend an entire weekend formatting a presentation to get the perfect fonts, with perfect animated sparkles at the perfect junctures. C'mon, does anyone really care? "It has to be perfect for the board of directors." Get real. The board of directors cares about the substance. They know how to add sparkles, they *don't* know the details of how the division is doing. Perfectionism is sucking up time, causing you to work more, and the only person benefitting is the owner of the company that wrote the presentation software. And he already has enough, don't you think?

Your presentations and reports don't need perfect formatting. Your product design doesn't need to be perfect, only better than the competition. Your spreadsheet doesn't need to have ten thousand cells calculating every possible interpretation of your data, only the interpretations that make a difference to how you'll move forward.

By now you agree you can lower your expectations from perfect to good enough. But who gets to define "good enough"?

If you're producing a product or service, good enough is defined by your customers. That's what market research is all about.

And if you want to do a good enough job to be promoted, it's your boss who can tell you what's good enough. It's true that your boss may define good enough differently from how the company defines it. I, however, shall diplomatically avoid a frank discussion of corporate politics and instead suggest that your All-Knowing, Benevolent Boss will happily help you understand how to do a good enough job.

Only never let your boss know you want to settle for good enough. Instead say, "What are the critical pieces that absolutely must get done; the things that we would never abandon even if our schedule slipped?" It's a simple question about priorities. Your boss will be thrilled to answer (unless she has never considered the question, in which case she'll feel threatened and fire you to resolve her uncomfortable feelings). It will also let you know what constitutes good enough, so you can relax once you've achieved those "good enough" requirements.

Now that you've dealt with finding what's good enough on the job, it's time to ramp down the extraperfectionism that's causing you more work with no benefit. Start finding where you strive for perfection. Do you format your documents obsessively? Do you go overboard on your community service? Do you try to be the perfect boss? Do you bow and scrape and say yes even when you mean no, in an attempt to be the perfect employee? List everywhere you're striving for perfectionism. For each, ask what would constitute "good enough"? Then, consider doing that. Use a table like the following one to help.

WHERE I'M A PERFECTIONIST	WHAT WOULD BE "GOOD ENOUGH"
Needing the perfect writing implement.	1 pen, 1 pencil.
Keep my computer backed up, totally updated, with multiple off-site backups.	Internet backup. Only do updates once a year.
Needing the podcast audio to be perfect before I send it to the sound engineer.	Send it immediately to the sound engineer. We pay *him* to make it perfect.

MAKE FASTER DECISIONS WITH ABSOLUTE LISTS

Now that you're working less by settling for good enough, let's take it down another notch and make it supereasy to know if something's good enough. Allow me to introduce Absolute Lists.* They come in two varieties: yes and no. An Absolute Yes list lays out the qualities that make an automatic yes for a decision. It tells you quickly what's good enough.

For example, I need a new car. I decide in advance if it costs less than $15,000, comes with a 100,000-mile warranty, gets over 35 miles per gallon, and is painted with a bigger-than-life picture of Elvis, I will buy it, no questions asked. (You may wish to ask why somebody would paint Elvis on their car, but I feel no such compulsion.)

This is my Absolute Yes list. If something matches everything on the list, it's an automatic yes. I take action and keep moving. Maybe there are things I would say yes to that don't match the list, but the list gives me a guaranteed cutoff. Anything matching

---

* I was first exposed to the ideas through Coach University and also through the work of author Cheryl Richardson.

instantly lets me proceed.* This makes life pretty easy. I don't have to spend a lot of time on things that fall in the gray area. If it's not an Absolute Yes, then it is a no.

You can use Absolute Yes lists to help you quickly recognize when to take a potential business deal seriously. You can create lists to help you screen job candidates, choose vendors, identify target customers, and choose the partners, companies, or bosses you want to work with. For example, if you're passionate about space travel and want the chance to be an astronaut someday, your Absolute Yes list for a job might include, "Provides the chance to travel to the moon." If you're passionate about space travel *and* housecleaning, you might include ". . . chance to travel to the moon and tidy things up once I'm there."

Once upon a time, if you had received a dozen job offers, you might agonize among them. You'd draw charts, evaluate pros and cons, and make the decision an agony of overwork. With your Absolute Yes list, you quickly scan through and realize that four of the jobs all involve space travel and housecleaning. Since all of them are an Absolute Yes, you can simply roll a four-sided die to make your final choice. A once-multiweek decision gets made in mere minutes.

We mostly try many options before we decide. Since we say no more times than we say yes, an Absolute No list can also help. The Absolute No list covers things that will instantly disqualify an option.

It's a very different creature from an Absolute Yes list. Sometimes you may not know exactly what you want in a job, but you *do* know that you despise fluorescent lights. An Absolute Yes list of "has flattering, incandescent lighting" won't do the job. Your office

---

* The academic scholar of decision theory will recognize this as "satisficing," a decision-making procedure named by psychologist Herbert Simon. Now that you've satisfied your desire for a citation, go finish reading the tip.

might have a single incandescent bulb in the customer waiting area, and then evil, soul-destroying fluorescent light everywhere else. But "no fluorescent lights" is an Absolute No. If a job also meets an Absolute No, thank them for the chance to apply and run as fast as you can, screaming, in the opposite direction.

You can use your Absolute Yes and Absolute No lists together. For example, when your friends (or family, or scout troup, or poly-amorous family unit) decide to catch a movie, you can easily end up spending all night debating what to see. Cut down the work by creating Absolute lists for the group to winnow down the choices quickly. Just fill out everyone's Absolute Nos. For your Absolute Yes list, include only criteria you *all* agree on. Instead of two hours of debate, just pull out your Absolute lists and elimi-nate any movies that trigger an Absolute No. If any movies trig-ger an Absolute Yes, go for it. Otherwise, you'll still have to discuss, but you've already eliminated all the noncontenders in mere moments.

TOPIC: MOVIES THE GROUP WANTS TO SEE	
Absolute Yes These are *group* absolute yeses.	**Absolute No** One person's absolute no is a veto.
Anything written by David Mamet	Gory horror (any villain wearing a ski mask, long fingernails, or who has stringy hair)
Star Wars franchise	Starring Madonna
Star Trek franchise	Starring anyone whose last name is the name of a hotel chain
Starring Meryl Streep, Matt Damon, or Pee Wee Herman	Anything with subtitles

Your Absolute lists will come in handy when making all kinds of tough decisions you face in your work life, including:

- Deciding whether or not to take on a new project.
- Evaluating whether or not to hire a prospective new team member.
- Deciding whether or not to stay late in the office to work on a project.
- Which interruptions get an immediate response (my vote is: none but life-or-death)?
- Whether you should spend money on a morale-building event.
- Whether you should spend money on a business-building event.

Here are how you might use Absolute lists around a business-building event:

TOPIC: BUSINESS-BUILDING EVENTS, SHOULD WE ENGAGE?	
Absolute Yes	**Absolute No**
It will provide guaranteed exposure to at least 1,000 people at a maximum cost of $15/person.	If it involves any explicit or implied political endorsement.
Trade shows for industries with cumulative sales of over $2 billion.	Anything that requires more than 10 people present (we don't yet have the staff to have that many people gone at once).
In past years, this event has led directly to sales or to valuable distribution partnerships.	Events held wherever we're on the "do not allow on premises" list (e.g. the Ballagio, after the unfortunate penguin incident).

You can also make Absolute lists for areas in your personal life:

- Whether or not to say yes when someone asks you on a date.
- Choosing a car.
- Deciding on a school to send your kids, or yourself.

What happens when an option you're considering meets both an Absolute Yes and an Absolute No? In that case, you have to fall back on thinking. There's no one answer. If you get the chance to sweep up the moon, in a spacesuit with fluorescent lighting, you need to decide whether the Absolute Yes of cleaning the lunar landscape is more or less important than your desire to be doing it under flattering conditions.

Just remember that you change over time. Once, marketing and sales scared me. Any job that required sales was an Absolute No. After years of self-employment, sales and I have made our peace, and it's fallen off the Absolute No list. Review your lists occasionally to make sure they're still correct. Well-thought-out Absolute lists help you make better decisions, far faster, so you can get on with acting, rather than deciding.

DON'T CONSIDER ALL OF YOUR OPTIONS

Absolute lists help us keep committed to "good enough," so we can quickly weed out bad options or jump right on good options. But they don't help with the other big decision time waster: getting caught between options. The more options we have, the more we get paralyzed in the middle. We feel overwhelmed and choose nothing. Three choices seem to be about what most of us can handle.

For proof, try buying shaving cream. You'll find sensitive skin cream, aloe-infused cream, moisturizing cream, gel cream, foaming cream, and little cakes of soap. You'll find shaving cream for pimply teenagers, shaving cream for monastic tonsure-wearing monks, shaving cream that can be applied under acceleration, and shaving cream that's specific to different body parts. I want it all! I want to be moist, gel-like, foaming, *and* covered with aloe. But that choice doesn't exist. Grabbing the first can in sight doesn't work, either. It turned out to be a brightly colored canister of spray-on hair dye. *Oops.*

Now imagine a world with just three choices for shaving cream: red, blue, and yellow. I choose blue because it's my favorite color. I'm rewarded with goose bumps of joy!

You can get goose bumps, too—and not just when buying shaving cream. When faced with an overwhelming number of options, find ways to limit your options.

Make an initial decision. Just do it, and you can ignore lots of the other options. A quick decision does mean you might miss the Perfect Choice. Ignore that. Life isn't about perfection, it's about living *outside* the shopping center.

Next time you shop for shaving cream, or laser printers, or portfolio covers, or gel-ink pens, look only at the top shelf. Ignore the rest. Arbitrary? Yes. But it limits your options and the decision gets easier.

Or decide about an important criterion: You'll only buy file folders that come in packs of eight colors and you'll ignore the rest. My printer paper decisions are easy. I buy recycled, twenty-four-pound paper. Voila! My choices narrow to one or two brands since most brands don't come in both recycled and twenty-four-pound versions.

I'm buying a car. I decide to limit my choices to "reasonable" gas mileage. Since my definition of "reasonable" starts at forty-five miles per gallon, my choices narrow quite nicely. At work, I'm choosing a vendor to rebuild our Web site from two hundred proposals submitted through our Web site. I decide to limit myself to only proposals that followed the outline we asked them to follow. (If they can't follow a simple outline, what are the chances they'll actually deliver the Web site we need?)

Limiting your choices can really come in handy when looking for a new job. Job seekers say, "I just want a challenging job that pays well." Casting such a wide net paralyzes them because there are too many avenues to begin.

Often just a few categories matter: the industry, what they'll be doing on the job, the city, and the specific company culture. Some people care about none of these; they just want a job. Others care about location, but not industry. Still others care about industry, job, *and* city.

The choice only becomes manageable by putting a stake in the ground and arbitrarily choosing. If you only care about living in Baltimore, for example, choosing an industry anyway and searching within that industry will make it a lot easier to find a job. Then if you don't find one, you can always try another industry. The more you limit, the easier it is to make progress.

Think of a choice where you're paralyzed by choice.

Identify the choice parameters. For choosing a job, it might be geography, industry, job function. For a car, it might be price, mileage, and sex appeal. For choosing a project, it might be who you would work with, how much work it would take, how much it would help you toward your goals (your desired work-less-to-progress-created ratio), and how many legs are on the food you have to eat in the village where the project takes place.

Arbitrarily choose some of the parameters. Use those choices to limit your options. For example, you might consider only cars that were driven by hot movie stars in 1980s action flicks. Now decide within this narrower set of options.

If none of the options are appealing, change your arbitrary decisions and try again. Maybe this time, you'll drop the sex appeal and instead choose based on gas mileage. Your Absolute lists can help here, since they work by making it fast and easy to narrow your choices. By limiting your choices and not considering every possibility, making decisions will be easier, and you'll keep moving forward.

DON'T WASTE TIME ON THE SMALL STUFF

Up to now, we've concentrated on the Trusty 20 that makes the most difference. The little stuff—the remaining 80 percent—makes a difference, too, even though it doesn't give you results. This may seem obvious, but it's really important. Expense reports must be filled out, papers filed, and staplers refilled. Even though it doesn't move you forward, it can sure hold you back if it gets neglected; small stuff matters.

Imagine a beautiful, antique clock with thousands of spinning gears and little levers. Open it and stick in a tiny twig. *Boom!* The clock stops working. But one look inside reveals the twig. It's an obvious problem. Pull it out, and everything's fixed.

Now, open the clock and toss in a handful of powder. The clock stops, but all we see inside is powder. It requires cleaning every nook and cranny separately. A handful of powder does more damage than a big stick in the clockwork.

In your life, there's the big stuff. You get abducted by aliens, used for medical experiments, and replaced by an android. That's an obvious problem. The less obvious problem is the little stuff. The tape dispenser melted to the desk again—yes, they do that. The accounting department spelled your name wrong on your paycheck and it bugs you every time the check arrives.

Any one thing isn't a big deal, but as a group, they become a drag on your life. They slow you down, take tiny bits of attention, and are a constant low-level distraction that keep you from getting into your groove. In the coaching world, we call these "tolerations," because . . . you tolerate them. They're not bad enough to fix, so you tolerate them, not realizing that together, they're like quicksand in your life. But if you clean them up, you will find yourself running free through fields of daisies. Who wouldn't want that?

The idea is simple, the execution, profound. Put this to work for yourself:

List ten things you are currently tolerating. List the small stuff. The fact that your parents just called to announce they're moving in? Not a toleration—that's the kind of thing that makes you drop out of sight and establish a new identity. I'm talking about the small stuff.

Grab your calendar. Schedule the next ten days. Each day, commit to taking care of one toleration.

When you've completed the ten days, notice how light your life feels.

Repeat the exercise until you have cleaned up everything you are tolerating.

THE NUMBER ONE RULE TO NOT WASTE TIME: BE PREPARED

One of my personal tolerations is also a huge time waster: I'm always hunting for the little things in life. Like my cell phone charger cord. Or lip balm. I have spent weeks of my life searching for lip balm. Not in the stores, but in my jacket. Halfway to a black tie fund-raiser with Very Important People, I realize my lips are like parchment paper. If they see that, they'll ostracize me forever. So I leave work early to run home, praying for lip balm. Instead of using the last thirty minutes of my workday to finish the Web site marketing copy that was top-of-mind, I'm fixated on cherry chapstick. It'll take me thirty minutes to get back into the Zone tomorrow, and a quick update that was going to be half an hour of work is now an hour—not to mention the wasted time my lip balm sprint took. This is *not* working less!

I spend *forever* looking for little things. As a geek, I must bring pens when I travel. There's a blue pen for signing contracts, the black gel pen for my to-do list, and the red pen in case someone asks me to grade homework. And let's remember my .5 mm mechanical pencil, in case I need to write something erasable.

When you need things in many different places, rather than trying to remember to carry them around, just buy several. My desk, satchel, and notebook all have extra pens. There are umbrellas at work, home, the car, my gym locker, by the front door, and by my desk. I buy them at the super-cheap discount store for three dollars apiece. I buy ten at once and am *never* caught high and dry—er, wet. Fire extinguishers hover within arm's reach on every floor. My gym locker has extra socks, gym shorts, T-shirts, and even underwear. (No, bachelors, one pair of underwear will *not* last for three weeks. Launder often!)

Think about the little things you're always forgetting to carry everywhere. Now, buy extras. My office and work areas are chock-full of extra sticky pads, paper clips, and even copies of my favorite reference books. Notebooks abound. And phone lists! We mustn't forget copies of my phone lists that live in my phone, my shoulder bag, my desk drawer, and my bulletin board.

I used to go crazy remembering to bring my phone charger with me on days I knew my phone use would be heavy. Then I got chargers for the car, the bedroom, the living room, and the office. Anywhere my phone goes, it knows it's never too far from a meal (though, remember to unplug the AC adapters; they use power even when the phone isn't plugged in).

By having extras, my work never gets interrupted by a sudden unexpected trip to the store to buy some small item. Once I'm in the Zone, everything will be at my fingertips when it's needed.

With a tiny bit of forethought and a shopping trip I'd take anyway, everywhere I go has all the resources I need and I'm working faster.

When you waste time, you're just throwing work away. When you're wasting the time playing a massively multiplayer online fantasy adventure, you know you're wasting time. That you can take care of on your own. Learning to identify your Trusty 20 gives you most of your results, turning down inappropriate perfectionism, and streamlining all the tiny time wasters in your life, you'll be able to streamline useless wheel-spinning and put your effort where it's bound to give you real results.

DON'T WASTE TIME ON MEETINGS

We've covered the general principles of not wasting time, but there's one specific, insidious practice that can't quite be tamed with the principles we've discussed so far. That's because it's a group waste-of-time, and thus not fully under your control. Yes, you guessed it. I'm talking about meetings. Anyone who wants to work less and do more must learn to make meetings productive, when running them and when being a victi—participant. Since taming meetings is key to not wasting time, we're going to close this chapter with a very special window into how you can control the inner workings of meetings and quietly bend them to your will.

Meetings *sound* terribly useful. Yet they are often poorly run, waste time, and do little but generate new "action items" that may or may not move your projects forward.

These time sucks have become the Swiss Army knife of business. Have a problem? Call a meeting! In business school, whenever one of my classmates wanted to score points without actually saying anything of substance, they would propose calling a meeting. "We'll just sit right on down and solve things. Shucks, it'll be *easy*!" Surely

cont'd

a meeting can fix anything. Unfortunately, this is one Swiss Army knife whose blade is dull.

Know exactly why you're calling your meeting before you call it and exactly what you want to get out of it. Then you know what you're trying to accomplish, and you can liberate everyone from meeting bondage as soon as you're done. They will head back to their offices, dazzled by the notion of actually getting stuff done, and you'll look like a hero. Everyone will bow down before you and life will be wonderful.

LOSE THE MEETING TO STOP WASTING TIME

Before you start trying to run faster meetings, figure out if you actually need to have the meeting in the first place. There are several types of meetings companies commonly have that can actually be eliminated entirely:

The Status Meeting is an information-sharing meeting. These meetings are almost entirely obsolete. You can replace them with an e-mail distribution list, a Wiki, a bulletin board, or one-on-one conversations. If you must have one, make sure you know why everyone's there, what each person will say, and why everyone else needs to know. That way, no one will have to work more and do less by sitting through a presentation that isn't relevant to them.

Decision-making meetings can be a horror show, since people can disagree with the goals of a decision, with the alternatives, and with the criteria being used to choose—in other words, the process part of decision-making. Take the process offline. Talk with people one-on-one about goals, alternatives, and criteria. At the actual meeting, agree to the goal, alternatives, and criteria as a group, or tweak them as needed (it won't be needed if you've done your prework). Then just evaluate your options and choose.

Team-building meetings assume that people who suffer through shared boredom will bond. If you want to team-build, go out to lunch together or do something everyone will enjoy. And please don't assume everyone loves football, golf, the outdoors, and cigars. Lunch will do just fine.

CHAPTER RECAP

- Stop wasting time by making sure what you're doing is work.

- Identify the 20 percent of your tasks that give you 80 percent of your results. Do more of those.

- Settle for "good enough" rather than wasting time on unnecessary perfection.

- Use Absolute Yes/No lists and limited choices to streamline your decision-making around "good enough."

- Limit your options and eliminate the tolerations that create a general drag on your energy.

- Buy several so you don't waste time hunting for the small stuff.

STEP 7

OPTIMIZE

I have some scary-yet-exciting news for you. Now that you're clear about your goals, you've eliminated distractions, you're focused and organized, and you're not wasting time, there's no other way to work less and get more done. Unless you change what you're doing and that's why step 7 is to optimize so you don't make the same mistake twice. There are many ways to do everything. Some ways take less work to get the same results. Most of my life could be done more effectively. It's probably true for you, too—you could find ways to do your same tasks that take less work and give more results. (If you already do everything perfectly, don't tell me! My ego couldn't handle it.)

Once upon a time, a CEO coaching client was speaking with her executive team. Every time someone made a suggestion that wasn't exactly what she wanted to hear, she would give a piercing glare, raise her voice, and repeat her point. Later, she complained that her executives weren't bringing up good ideas. I suggested perhaps she needed a new way of listening. She sighed, gave me a piercing glare, and proclaimed, "I said, my *executives* aren't earning their pay." She fell right into the same pattern with me that she used with her executives . . . and never heard the answer she needed.

We humans are built funny. We do the same thing over and over, even if it doesn't work. We love what's *familiar* more than we love getting what we want. In college, my friend Chris scored poorly on tests. I scored well. We compared our study habits and realized they were very different. We agreed to study my way for our next test. A few days before, however, he abandoned our study sessions to return to his method. He explained, "Even though your way might work better, mine just feels more comfortable." He prepared the same way and got the same results—a poor grade.

In this chapter, we'll move beyond what's familiar in search of what's better. It's easy to find, if you know the steps. First, we'll get rid of what isn't working, so we'll have the time to optimize the rest of what we do. Then we'll learn lazy ways to find where we can improve what we do. We'll find lazy ways, because we certainly don't want to do more work than necessary, even when we're finding ways to save time. Then we'll create many alternatives that give us the same results with less work. And last, we'll build learning directly into our systems so they optimize themselves while we lie in our hammock, sipping fruit-flavored beverages, eating Oreo ice cream cake.

OPTIMIZE BY GETTING RID OF OUTDATED PRODUCTIVITY SYSTEMS

Let's start optimizing by saying "bye-bye" to the productivity systems you've outgrown. Let's use me as an example. I'm super-organized! I color code every cable in my office in colors ranging from aquamarine to puce. It feels *very* productive, and lets me feel superior to all those poor souls who don't color code their cables. There's only one problem. I've never actually used the color coding to figure out what a cable does or where it goes. My love of productivity has slipped into codependence, and my organizing system itself is wasting my time. From here on in, no more cable color coding because it's not helping me do anything but work more, not less.

My time-wasting systems weren't limited to color coding cables. For fifteen years, I organized my finances on computer, first by spreadsheet, then with a software program. Every receipt was categorized. Every statement balanced, and every account reconciled to the penny. Not once did I *ever* print a report, or use that information to understand my spending. I did, however, spend months of my life typing receipts and thousands of dollars upgrading software.

I hired a bookkeeper and trashed the personal finance program. The bookkeeper is more expensive, but the *weeks* I save each year are well worth it.

I'm sure you have systems in your life that may no longer be serving you. Mentally scan your life and notice where you're disorganized and where you aren't. Here's a list of places in your life to jog your memory.

File folders	Reading articles	Receipt tracking
Scheduling	Saving e-mail newsletters	E-mail inbox
Cooking	Hanging clothing	Camping
Writing reports	Doing laundry	Throwing parties
Reading reports	Shopping for food	Keeping your computer running
Preparing for travel	Traveling	
Doing taxes	Handling medical bills	

For each organized area, estimate the savings to being organized. If it takes more effort or more time to organize than to be messy, stop using the organization system. Breathe a sigh of relief and treat yourself to a tasty stalk of celery stuffed with hummus. Yum!

For each disorganized area, estimate what disorganization is costing you in time and money. If it's costing a lot, *that* is where to put your organizing time and effort. In short: When having a system *doesn't* help you work less, feel free to drop it.

USE FEEDBACK TO OPTIMIZE

Now that your familiar-but-useless organization systems are out of the way, you'll have some breathing room. Your next step to working even less is to find where in your life you can do things differently. I wouldn't recommend looking, however, since that would involve work. Instead, let the universe point the way.

Of course, by "the universe," I mean those helpful people who are just *full* of helpful hints on how you can improve. They call it "feedback." We can see right through them. Nothing could be more obvious than their deep-seated need to combat their own sense of inadequacy by offering us all that helpful help. But that doesn't mean their feedback isn't helpful; it is! It tells us where we could be working less and getting more done.

When I was a kid, the other kids, in their caring, offered feedback. They said, "You're ugly," and "You're some kind of space alien!" Their helpful feedback led me to buy nose-hair clippers, get a haircut, and spend sixty thousand dollars on therapy for my alien-abduction issues. My therapist says I'm unique since my delusions are from the alien point of view.

Now I'm sure this has happened to you. Your boss gives helpful feedback. "Your report looks like it was typed by a monkey."

Or "Gee, your presentation was well thought out! . . . for a change."
It feels . . . horrible.

Even the people who try to give good feedback usually can't
pull it off to save their lives. So count on feedback coming in
every unpleasant, obnoxious way you can imagine. You'll only
be happy if you learn to hear what they're saying, no matter
how poorly they say it. And trust me, you want to hear it. They
may have noticed what you can optimize so you do more, working less.

Defensiveness is the signal that you've found a place you
could do something differently. If someone says "You're a fake!"
you might jump up and down, clenching your fist, yelling, "Me?
A fake? I knew the whole time *your* shoes weren't real Prada!"
When you're reduced to insulting footwear, it's a sign you're being defensive. Back up and notice the feeling right before the
defensiveness. You felt attacked. Maybe you tighten your chest,
squint slightly, and tense up. Learn the feeling. It's your new
signal. It tells you someone's "helpful" feedback has hit home.
Once you feel it, find it.

You only feel defensive when you agree at some level with
what they say. I never wore braces. Call me tinsel teeth and I'll
think you're nuts. But I *did* wear glasses. Call me four-eyes, and
my gut yells, "No I'm not!" That hurts. And it's stupid, because
sure, I *am* four-eyed; I wear glasses and was apparently a space
alien. We feel most defensive about things we fear might be true.

Once you feel it, *find it.* No matter how outrageous or strange,
go inside and genuinely find a way it is or was true for you. But
do it without blame, shame, or guilt! Just find the truth and
notice. My nemesis says, "You dress weird." Do I? People *do* get
funny expressions when I show up at business meetings in a skin-
tight vinyl vest and sequined pants. So, yes, I can see how they
might think that. And when I find it, the defensiveness lets go.
Now we agree, and I feel no need to attack.

This new knowledge helps me dress better. That way, my colleagues spend their time giving me what I need to get my job done, instead of gossiping behind my back. I can only work less if everyone else is giving me what I need, instead of commenting uselessly on my sequined platform shoes. Which are perfectly stylish on the planet I come from. Coworkers may give you more constructive feedback than commenting on your pants. Bernice might say, "Your reports are poorly formatted, and your phobia of punctuation makes them hard to read."

If you go inside and don't find their criticism, fine. Now you know how they perceive you and can ask for details. You might reply, "What in the world *are* you talking about it makes no sense to me could you explain *what* do you mean my phobia of *punctuation* makes them hard to read?" Then they might help you understand their point. They become your teacher, not your enemy. Are you fooling yourself by assuming their feedback is right? Maybe. But if you fool yourself into staying calm and learning something, I say, embrace self-deception. It's good practice if you ever want to run for office.

Once you've found where their feedback could be accurate, consider what would happen if you followed up by changing what you do. Would the change make less work? Would it help you get more done? Then for goodness' sake, do it! People said my memos were too detailed and hard to follow. Threatened, I prepared to tie them down and tattoo "Stever is an awesome writer" on their forehead. Since tattoo fantasies almost always signal incoming criticism, I took a deep breath and reread my report, to find their criticism. Sure enough, my memos were *really* detailed. Someone who didn't know the material *would* find it confusing. I rushed right out and grabbed a book on how to structure good business writing. (For information on the book I used, see this book's resource Web site.) Learning to write with less detail meant saving on typing, the amount of work I put in, and more people actually reading my brilliant reports.

By learning to accept the criticism no matter how poorly it was delivered, it helped me better understand what was needed. Next time I could work less by writing the way my audience needed the first time around. Soon, I was writing with the prose.°

Once you've found the truth, follow up on it. If they say your fonts are weird, ask them for formatting help. If they call you four-eyes, you can even say, "You're right. I do have four eyes. Do you think Lasik would help?" This works with any criticism. "Your report is shallow and stupid." "Really? Can you help me understand what I've missed?" "You didn't deliver what the team needed." "That's not how I saw it. Can you share your side with me?"

You don't have to take their advice. Just ask, listen, and consider it for real. What makes this work is your honest effort to hear it. Here are a couple of true-life examples.

A job seeker hears: "You just don't seem to be the right fit for this."

Could it be? If they're saying it, maybe so. Now follow up and ask, "Can you help me understand the fit?" And by the way, if you're smart, you do want to know. Ending up in a job that's a bad fit leads to misery. If you want to get a job quickly, this could be the information that can help you do better in your next application.

A coworker tells Butch: "The way you interrupted people in the meeting to make your point really annoyed them. You need to work on your people skills."

Butch bursts into tears, and knows tears signal a message worth listening to. Butch finds it: Are my people skills a tad rusty? Well, there was that time Butch gave the boss helpful tips about

---

° Of course the pun is intentional. It's the highest form of humor, as long as you're standing on your head.

those ugly, ugly shoes in the middle of explaining the new procedures for filling out status reports. Then there were the jokes about Bernice's weight that came right after explaining how to more efficiently draft a memo. In fact, at last week's team meeting, everyone took turns sticking pins into a little wax Butch doll. At the time, Butch assumed it was an acupuncture demonstration. But now it takes on a whole new meaning. Butch realizes that it is, indeed, a good idea to develop better people skills. Maybe then they'll listen to his points the first time so he won't have to waste time saying the same thing over and over again at every meeting.

OPTIMIZE BY GETTING EXPERT HELP

When you've found something to optimize, like how to share your point of view during a meeting, the next step is finding other ways to do the same thing with less work. An easy way to find other ways to get stuff done is to ask someone who has the expertise to help. It may be a friend, a coworker, a family member, or a Get-It-Done Guy. Choose an expert to help, but be sure to choose your expert wisely.

We believe experts know what they're talking about. We think they can give us the steps to bring us to the same land of milk and honey they live in.

There are two problems. First, milk and honey just isn't the delectable taste treat you might think. Second, an expert's advice will only work for you if they started from the same place as you, are pursuing the same goals, and have strategies that can work in *your* life. They'll also tell you what they *think* worked, and there's no reason to believe they know. Many successful "experts" succeeded *in spite of* what they did, not because of it!

Think about the people you automatically admire based on the size of their . . . mansion. Ask yourself how much of their success was luck, timing, and being born to the right parents. If they're an incompetent boob who happened to be born with a trust fund, they're not your source. When you find someone who you believe has actual skill, they're an expert you might consult to learn to do whatever you're doing with less work and get greater results.

You're not looking for someone who can do things better than you; you want someone who can help *you* get better results. You don't choose a mentor because *they* are doing great; you choose a mentor who will coach *you* to do *your* job easier, quicker, faster, with better results. Top coaches aren't top players; they bring out the best in *any* player we give them. It's the same for advice givers. Their product isn't their own excellence, it's yours.

Before going to an expert for advice, check out their students. Meet people they have taught, worked with, or supervised who started from the same place as you. If you've figured out that mastering communication skills will help you do more going forward with *way* less effort, don't look for people with superb communication skills. Look for the ones who taught them! Find the ones who have turned *other* people from pocket-protector-wearing stereotypes into suave secret agents who can charm even the most evil supervillain.

The best experts to help you find better ways of doing things actually change your thinking so you get better even when you're no longer with the expert. They make new distinctions you hadn't been aware of. My mild-mannered boss Billy (name changed in case his undercover CIA identity is blown) was that kind of teacher.

Billy is quiet, unassuming, and a really nice person. From our first group meeting, where I put my foot carefully into my mouth and swallowed it all the way up to the midthigh, he took me under his wing to teach me how to survive in a big organization. I'm one of those nerds who always believed everyone had good intentions and were all working for the common good. He helped me realize that people—however sincere and well meaning—all have their own concerns and priorities. They may also have the power to thwart me. Now I enter a meeting and a control screen appears in my mind. It shows everyone's agendas, color coded by alliance. Remaining hit points glow in red or green numbers over their head. Rather than spending weeks, months, or years fighting people who stall my Grand Plans That Will Revolutionize Everything, I now have all the information I need to help everyone else meet their needs, so they'll support mine when the time comes.

Billy is an expert who gave me fundamental new distinctions about the world. Those distinctions let me get far more done because people no longer fight me. I realize my job isn't just reaching my own goals, but helping everyone around me reach theirs, while dodging the fire bolts and stun spells of the wizards on the opposing team.

(I, of course, am an expert who meets all of the above criteria perfectly. My every word is perfect, applies perfectly to your situation, helps you make new distinctions, and will lead you to the land of lasagna and Oreo ice cream cake, both of which are tastier than milk and honey.)

OPTIMIZE BY LISTENING TO YOURSELF

Along with your outside experts, you have another expert: You. We're all experts when it's not about us. When our friend, husband, wife, spousal equivalent, or polyamorous family unit has a problem, we're front and center with a solution. A perfect solution, by the way. And no matter how much they protest, we know their life would be so much easier if only they would listen to us.

And therein lies the secret to making *our* lives better. That oh-so-important advice we give them is actually the advice we should give *ourselves*. That's the cosmic joke: We know how to make our lives better. We just give the advice to everyone but us, and get outraged when they share *their* wisdom with us.

When you're tempted to give advice, zip it. Think about what you would say and give *yourself* the advice instead. It might not translate directly, but I assure you, it will translate. You've found a part of life that could be easier, and you've even figured out *how* it could be easier. That you found it in someone else's life is an irrelevant detail.

For example, one of my special powers is noticing when other managers could run better meetings. I notice Akbar holds meetings without agendas, has no defined goals, and sends the team off to do absurd research whose results aren't relevant moving forward. I'm happy to tell Akbar how much better life would be by taking my advice. Then I walk into my own team meeting, having forgotten to prepare an agenda, not recalling our goal from last week, and asking the team to "study the problem further" while I desperately try to get my bearings. If only someone had some good advice on how to prepare for a meeting. Oh. That would be me. Maybe next time I lecture Akbar, I'll listen first.

If you think, "Bernice should keep a neater desk," look around for the chance for *you* to be neater. If you think, "Akbar should keep on top of his schedules," you might think to recheck yours. You learned in "Step 5: Stay Organized" that being organized in desk and mind frees up all the time you used to spend hunting for what you need. Now that it's top-of-mind, instead of thinking about Bernice or Akbar, look at yourself again to find out if you're as organized as you could be. You'll be surprised how much you already know about where and how *you* can optimize your life to work less and do more. You just express it as advice to others, instead of yourself. Take my advice: Take your own advice.

OPTIMIZE WITH A LEARNING LOG

Since we're all about working less, it would be foolish to have to learn the same lessons more than once. Doing something more than once drives me nuts, even something as fun as learning. Make a mistake once, shame on me. Make a mistake twice, well, shame on me again. And I don't like being shamed on twice.

Marla, a very successful woman, was my mentor in high school. She passed on sage words of advice: Keep a diary. Every evening, write down what you learned that day. Reflect, and learn from your life. When someday you want to streamline your life, you can browse through your learning log and discover you've learned dozens of lessons that could help you reach your goals and just needed a reminder.

Remember that experts aren't always right, and in this case, you are your own expert. When you jot down a lesson, be skeptical. Ask, "Does this apply elsewhere in my life? Or was it a one-shot thing?" Capture your learning, but before you use it, make sure you believe it applies throughout your life.

I capture my learning in a learning log that I keep on a spreadsheet. Column one is the lesson I've learned, so I can read it by scanning the first column. I just type in, "Always hold an anteater by the hindquarters when combing its snout." After dozens and dozens of tips accumulate, however, it gets hard to find tips easily.

The second column comes to the rescue. There, I add phrases and words that will jog my memory. For example, I would enter "anteater, animal, pet behavior, grooming, and thumb-reattachment incident" into the cell next to the anteater tip.

To find a lesson, just search for the most likely and relevant keywords. If those keywords aren't in the tip itself, they will often be found in the reminder column. For example, if you're bringing in a new team member, you search for "orientation" or "team building." The search then reveals tips about defining roles and responsibilities, helping someone feel welcome, introducing a new team member, and so on. Instead of reinventing your orientation procedure every time someone joins, your learning log gives you instant, effortless access to everything you've learned about bringing in a new teammate.

On days you don't learn anything, call a friend and find out what they learned. Why just learn from your own experience? Learn from *their* pain. It's so much more comfortable. Besides, you'll be doing them a favor since you're giving them an excuse to reflect on their day as well.

Tip	Key words
Hold an anteater by the hindquarters when combing its snout.	anteater, comb, grooming, snout, thumb-reattachment incident
Send flowers to repair a social relationship. Do not do this at work; it can be misconstrued!	flowers, amends, apologies, restraining order
Define roles and responsibilities at the start of each project.	project, management, teams, interpersonal, process
Give everyone else the credit; over time, people will notice if you're always the manager.	leadership, credit, rewards, morale, management

USE YOUR TO-DO LIST TO OPTIMIZE

So far, you've still put in work learning. If you want to work even *less*, you can use your existing systems to help with learning or to make it happen magically. Your existing systems can become a tool to delegate much of what you do to those who haven't yet learned to say no.

The most wonderful way to work less is to let someone else do your work for you. But it's hard, because you have to figure out what to tell them to do. Let your to-do list do the thinking for you. We usually think our to-do list is a tool to control the future, but it's also a handy diary.

For the next week, save your to-do lists. If you do something not on your list, add it and then check it off. You'll feel deep satisfaction from all that checking off, but more importantly, you'll have a list of everything you did during the week. You now have a summary of where your time is spent.

By each to-do item, note how much time you spent during the week on that item. Also jot down what skills or information someone would need to do that item for you.

To-do	Time	Skills/knowledge
Answer e-mail	10 hrs/week	Technical skills; familiarity with my job and responsibilities; ability to triage incoming issues
Clean bedroom	5 mins/day	Spatial reasoning; organizational skills; hazardous material suit
Drop Jed at baseball	3 hrs/week	Driving skills; availability to 3 p.m. daily
Call job candidates	1 hr/day	Knowledge of corporate culture; knowledge of job requirements; ability to assess broad skill level over phone

Now brainstorm how you can delegate as many items on your list as possible. You learned in step 6 that delegating is how you deal with your old job when your work gets redefined. When you're optimizing your job, you take delegation one step further: You use it as a tool for spreading your current work whenever possible to the person who can do it best. Delegation needn't always be to people who work for you. You can delegate to teenagers, consultants, or that nice young bard who is desperately vying for your hand and will do anything to earn your favor. Find delegatees and delegate, delegate, delegate! Your to-do list, far from being your taskmaster, is now the instrument of your liberation.

Your to-do list can go a step further; *it* can get smarter over time. When you do a task with many steps, like setting up a new distribution channel for your new line of gummy earth-moving equipment candy, write down a to-do list with all the steps and check them off as you do them. The to-do list becomes a template for future tasks. The next time you have to do the same thing, you won't waste time trying to remember all the ins and outs. Nor will you forget the most important step and waste time cleaning up your own mess. Instead, if your list learns from experience, you just lay back and sip margaritas while your list gets smarter and smarter.

To create a to-do list turned checklist, store the master copy of your list on your computer. At first, type in everything you think you might need to do to finish your project:

- call ten national distributors
- tell them jokes about earthmoving equipment
- ask them to buy the new candy

Make it a bulleted list with hollow circles. Print out the list and hang it by your desk. When you decide you *do* need to do a certain step while working on the project, draw a slash through the bullet next to the item so you know you're working on it. If a task comes up you have to do that isn't on the list, add it, draw in a little bullet, and put a slash through it.

If some new demand on your time appears, check your list. If a distributor calls asking to talk to you about your gummy machinery technical specs and completing technical specs is not already on your task list, add it with a slash, so you know it's a task you now must complete.

Make Your To-Do List Learn

When the project ends and it's time for your scheduled computer time, type in all the handwritten items you had to add that weren't on the list to start with. Then print out the new, fresh list. The whole process begins again when the next project starts up.

Your to-do list gradually becomes a project plan of everything you need to do to finish a certain kind of project. You can use it the next time this project comes up, or you can give it to your delegatees as an instruction manual, or leave it for the person who replaces you when you leave this job for your dream job taste testing Oreo ice cream cakes (or wait, maybe that's *my* dream job?).

OPTIMIZE YOUR GROCERY SHOPPING

The same concept behind turning to-do lists into checklists can also be used outside of the office for tasks like grocery shopping.

Let's say you hate grocery shopping. You always go when you're hungry, and you don't even bother to take a list. You just get what looks good. Like marinated olives. You constantly have two hundred half-eaten tubs of marinated olives in the fridge, and let's not get started on the string cheese. You need to set up a list that learns from experience.

cont'd

Your household probably shops for the same stuff every week. Maybe you change brands a bit. This week, you buy the sixteen-pack of Kleenex, while next week it's the sixteen-pack of Scott tissue. Over time, you'll realize your weekly shopping list should include a sixteen-pack of tissue paper. You will also realize you should see a nose doctor about that. It's not normal.

You hang the list on the fridge. Everyone knows to draw a slash through the bullet when you need something. Take the paper list when you head to the store and buy the items with slashes. If you see a canister of Zombie Reanimation Powder and remember you need it, just toss it into the cart. If it was already on the list without a slash, "X out" the bullet. Then when you get home, find whoever used the last package and make their life a living heck for not having marked it off on the sheet. Life is too short not to torture your loved ones into making *your* life more convenient. Of course, if it wasn't even on the list to begin with, add it—and any other new products you bought—when you get home. Then print out the new, fresh list, and put it on your bulletin board. The whole process starts again.

The key to making this work is that your list gradually becomes a list of pretty much everything you ever might need. Then it becomes everyone's responsibility to notice when you actually *do* need something. If one of your loved ones hassles you for forgetting an item, you can thrust the responsibility right back at them. Smile sweetly and say, "You didn't add it to the list." Then make *them* go out and get it, immediately. Soon, people will learn it's much easier to keep the bulletin board list up-to-date than to be running out for Zombie Reanimation Powder every time. Those days of wasting time wandering aimlessly through the aisles will be long gone.

For extra credit, group items on your list by their supermarket aisle. If you're as pathetic as I am, you can even put the aisles in the same order on your sheet as they are in the store. So when you head out to shop, you just zip through the items grabbing what you need.

And that, my friend, makes shopping a joy. Well, not a joy. But less of a soul-rending agony of remembering your list, and navigating your cart, and time, and space, and multidimensional teleportation.

USE RESOURCE BOOKS TO OPTIMIZE ANY NEW TASK

Now we're going to put together the idea of a to-do list that learns with a learning log. A to-do list only tracks tasks, and a learning log only tracks lessons that you find through Daily Deep Thought. When you do something for the first time, use that as a chance to record, remember, and automate everything associated with the job in a resource book.

If you adopt a new job responsibility, like overseeing your company's honey-harvesting operation, start optimizing your first day on the job. Get a notebook that will become your resource book, and record everything you do, moment by moment, as you learn the tricks of the trade. Also record the lessons you learn, and the resources you'll use. If there's an emergency honey-removal service you need to call, record it in the resource book. If you need certain information—like the airspeed velocity of a European honeybee-eating swallow—record it in the resource book. Also keep the contact information for people you meet while running down the street chased by a swarm of angry bees. Your notebook becomes a to-do list and resource list for your second day on the job (just as soon as the swelling goes down). It's similar to a learning log, but you don't just record your lessons, you record all the resources, names, account numbers, and everything else needed to do the task.

Create this resource book the first time you do something. Then treat it like a to-do list that learns. As you continue the work over time, change your resource book if phone numbers change, or if new steps get added to the process (like realizing you should insert step 3a, "put on protective suit before entering hive"). Your resource book becomes a living reference and instruction manual for doing the job. Not only is it a guide for you next time, but it becomes a ready-made delegation tool to train someone else.

Your resource book can even become a promotional product! When I first began podcasting, I obsessively carefully recorded every setting on my recording equipment, and every step of how I processed the sound, eliminated noise, and made it sound good. Eventually my podcast recording resource book became a permanent page on my Web site, because so many people asked how it was possible to get such great sound out of a home studio. What makes a resource book so valuable is that it includes not only the steps for a task, but all the extra information you need while you're doing the task.

This practice of creating task-specific resource books is one of the most useful habits I've ever adopted. It's supereasy, and every time you learn something, you end up with everything you need to do it again, delegate it, or write a book about it. How do you think I first gathered my wealth of information about creating Zombie armies?

Once you've taken care of all the outside forces that create work for you, the next step is to optimize by finding where you can get the same results with less work. Criticism from others and "advice" you give others will point toward the opportunities for improvement. Use experts—including yourself—to create the new options. Learn from your past experience, then work even less by delegating what you do that you're not best at, and tweaking your remaining systems so they improve themselves automatically.

CHAPTER RECAP

- Once you're focused and distraction-free, working less and doing more requires changing how you do things from the familiar to what's more effective.

- Find improvement opportunities by listening to outside feedback.

- Create alternatives by asking experts who have a track record of helping people.

- Listen to and follow the advice you give others, so you can optimize your life.

- Keep a learning log so the past you can give advice to the present you.

- Use your existing to-do list for delegation and make it learn so you don't have to.

- Create resource books as you learn a new task, so you have everything you could ever need at your fingertips.

STEP 8

BUILD STRONGER RELATIONSHIPS

At first glance you might be thinking, "What does building stronger relationships have to do with working less and doing more?" Working together is a time-honored way to get tons of stuff done faster, much more than one person can do on their own. One person alone can paint a beautiful mural on a wall. But if that person stands on another person's shoulders, they can also paint the moulding around the edges of the ceiling. I speak from personal experience.

Strong, vibrant relationships help you work less because people look out for one another. When you get stuck, the people you've developed strong relationships with will help you out. When you need to reach people on two hundred college campuses to get them involved in a nationwide competition, it's a lot of work. Unless you're good friends with the man who runs an organization with chapters at two hundred college campuses. Then you just walk into the next office and ask for a favor. Instead of spending the next six weeks calling student group after student group, having many diverse, deep connections can get you what you need in mere moments.

When you bring several of your strong relationships together to work on a project, you can divide the work so each person handles the thing they know best, resulting in all of you not getting stuck on a task above your expertise level and working better, faster. Together, you accomplish more than you ever could alone. That's why building strong relationships is step 8 in our quest to work less and do more.

Since I started life as a four-eyed geek with no friends, I learned to build relationships step-by-step. Now it's your turn. We'll be covering a couple of the highlights of my, er, twenty-five years of learning about people. We'll learn to deepen relationships, give people the gift that will endear them to us forever, and manage conflict on those rare occasions that things get rough, so we can reach our ultimate life of frolicking among the daisies, checking in for work but once a week to push the button labeled "Start."

AN IMPORTANCE-OF-RELATIONSHIPS FABLE

In case you need an example of the power of relationships and how they can help you have a huge impact with far less work, this fable is for you:

Once upon a time, a man was walking along a beach. In the distance, he saw a little girl. She was bending down and picking something up. Then she would throw it into the ocean, smile, and do it all again.

As he approached, he asked her, "What are you doing, little girl?"

"I'm saving this starfish that has been stranded here by the tide," she said as she picked up a starfish and threw it back into the ocean.

"But little girl," the man cried, "there are hundreds of stranded starfish on this beach alone. And there are thousands of beaches like this one. You can't make a difference by rescuing one starfish!"

The little girl smiled. She reached down, picked up a starfish, and hurled it into the ocean. "I made a difference to that one," she replied.

The moral of the story is admirable: Any action, no matter how small, can matter.

What an incredibly depressing moral. This devious story is actually an oppressive plot by our Secret Overlords to make us feel content with mediocre lives. "I made a difference to that one," indeed! Little girl, let me introduce you to the phenomenal power of relationships.

Let's try it again. Once upon a time, a man was walking along a beach. In the distance, he saw a thousand people scouring the beach.

He approached a little girl and asked, "What are you doing?"

"We're looking for stranded starfish to rescue," she explained.

"But there aren't any starfish here," the man replied.

"Then we've saved them all. Our work here is done," explained the little girl. She blew her whistle, and a thousand people piled back into a fleet of vans and started to drive away. As the first van turned out of the parking lot, he could read the brightly colored logo on the side, "Little Girl™ Starfish Rescue Service . . . over 1 billion starfish saved."

The little girl in the second story realized that great things happen when you have many strong relationships. When she heard about the starfish problem, she immediately called her ten BFFs. They posted signs around their school and had an official "Save the Starfish" event. Realizing she needed more people to care, she called the local TV station. Three months later, her PR efforts had gone national. With a thousand people joining the effort, she could make a real difference.

The man walked on, realizing the little girl had done more good in the world than he had in his thirty-five years as an actuarial accounting consultant. He looked down and saw a crab that had been washed into a tidal pool and needed rescuing. He turned and began to run back to the departing vans. "Wait! Guess what we can do together. . . ."

DON'T JUST BUILD RELATIONSHIPS, BUILD CLOSE RELATIONSHIPS

Relationships will help you work less and do more, but that doesn't mean the time you spend building your relationships is automatically time well spent. Relationships themselves take time to build. We often meet someone new, hit it off, and spend a dozen hours eagerly swapping stories about how we care for our man-eating boa constrictors. That's not enough! In fact, it may be a total waste of time, because a huge one-time marathon does *not* build a real relationship. Because this book is all about working less and doing more, I'm going to tell you how you can work less and do more when building connections and relationships. Once you've got those, they in turn will be the key to work less and do more in the life you're creating. Relationships take time, and we're on a quest to get the maximum bang from our time investment, just like dating.

I am horrible at dating. My Highly Successful Friend says you have to have "mystique" and leave people wanting more. Sadly, I'm not very "mystique-ious." I'm a reformed nerd; I'm kinda "what you see is what you get."

You can imagine my delight as an adult when I found out that networking, getting noticed at work, and sales were all just variants on dating, my worst-skill-ever.

As a kid, I made a few friends because we did lots of things together. We hung out at the mall playing video games, had

Cosmic Encounter tournaments, and dressed up in costumes from *Elfquest*. At slumber parties, we talked late into the night, uncovering deep philosophical truths. Did you know our entire universe might be a tiny atom in the fingertip of an unimaginably large creature . . . who's just about to put his finger up his nose? That mutual gasp of "Oooh, gross!" bonded us for a lifetime.

Stories of socially inept monsters no longer work. People don't have time to listen. Fortunately, building relationships doesn't depend on the stories. Strange to tell, but true. And it isn't love at first sight, either; that's lust. Love happens at fifteenth sight.

In this world of constant change, what sticks? It's the things that repeat. Ancient humans would chant songs and tell tales of great wisdom over and over to commit life lessons to memory. Me? I heard a Burger King commercial two thousand times and can list the ingredients of a Whopper with my eyes closed: Two all-beef patties, special sauce, lettuce, cheese, pickles, onions on a sesame seed bun. I *say* my brain is more advanced than my ancestors. Please, convince me it's an improvement.

The more someone encounters you and your name, the more they'll remember you. Let's say you want to work less when dealing with your vendors. You know from past experience that having a strong personal relationship with your contact at a vendor makes it easy to handle schedule changes with a simple phone call rather than an elaborate, bureaucratic negotiation.

You decide to begin building a relationship with Dorian, your new account rep. Find many small ways to interact. And though it may seem odd, when you're just starting to build a relationship with someone, less depth to the early conversations might be best. Mystique sells because it is essentially a lack of information. Without reality to go on, people project their fantasies, hopes, and dreams on you. They'll naturally project what they want you to be, then make friends with it. You don't have to do much at all. Just show up and smile (or frown, if they like their friends serious).

In these initial short conversations, find out something Dorian needs and then do him a small favor. Connect him with people he wants to meet. If you have mutual friends, ask your friends to mention you. Dorian will gradually build a you-shaped place in their mind. When you finally have that first in-depth conversation, you already have the memory hook and soon Dorian will be handling your schedule changes after only ten seconds on the phone.

A single contact won't make much of an impression. You need to connect several times to cement a relationship. Marketers know that it takes seven impressions to get someone to remember a product. Let's take a page from their book and adopt it here. When you want to begin building a relationship, find seven ways to get your name mentioned and to build positive associations with the person you're romancing. Help them with a problem, send them an article of interest, get their kids into the exclusive private school whose board you're on. Stuff like that. When you're contacting them seven times, you might even have time for a conversation or two. Choose topics that build closeness.

CUT OUT THE SMALL TALK

Let's face it: We don't have time for superficial relationships. If relationships will help us work less, we should choose the quickest way to building the strongest relationships. We bond over shared hardship, like being stranded in Antarctica for three years as we desperately try to hike four thousand miles and row to the nearest island. That requires physical discomfort, however, which is *really* low on my fun list. We also bond over conversation, though not just any conversation. And especially not small talk.

Many people make small talk to get to know someone. I don't

"get" small talk. Mine is so small it's invisible. "How's the weather?" asks the person I've just met at the conference buffet, as they try to slip an extra bacon-wrapped sardine into their pocket without anyone noticing. "It's quite cold," I say aloud. Inside, I'm thinking, "Yo, sardine-breath, look out the window for goodness' sake." *My* kind of icebreaker is, "Are you happy with your life, and how have you compromised your dreams and deepest desires to get here?" My popularity at cocktail parties is legendary.

I think small talk is a complete waste of time. The real way to build a relationship with someone is to create intimacy by moving your conversation up a ladder of intimacy. There's been research done on the topic, and since I'm not a scientist, I'm probably going to mangle it beyond belief. But even so, it may work for you. You can use these tips when going to networking events and more generally when you meet someone new whom you want to build a relationship with.

When asked a question, where does someone's attention go? They don't argue. They don't analyze. They try to find the answer. When you're talking with people, this is double-plus good. All you have to do is ask someone a really good question and they'll talk for hours. It saves you the effort of thinking; all you have to do is listen. Furthermore, people *love* talking about themselves. The more chance you give them to talk, the more they'll think *you* are a spectacular conversationalist.

Communication starts with agreement. You'd think this is obvious, but start building your relationship with flattery. Insults and instructions for how your new friend could improve do not build rapport. Bernice joined me for a party at my friend's apartment. I introduced her to our host. Her first words were, "Your walls are so bare. You should have more pictures." My host later confided that he was not yearning for a lifelong friendship with Bernice. He was, however, fantasizing about spilling red wine on her white linen dress and calling her names like "Strumpet."

Start your conversations with externalities and traits. Externalities are things about the environment, and traits are someone's characteristics. It's easy to find areas of agreement if you look at externalities and traits. Just make sure to bond over *positive* ones. You can be genuinely curious about an externality or trait. "What lovely walls. The lighting effects make it seem so spacious. How did you decide to do that?" (externality) Or, "Gee, you have red hair and blue eyes. Was your mother Irish?" (traits)

After externalities and traits, move up the ladder to discussing values. Values are what you hold as important in life. Your values might include: family, trust, connection, justice, love, cooperation, winning, enjoying the journey, wisdom, et cetera. Finding common values is a quick way to begin deepening a relationship.

A person's values are expressed through their goals. Remember in step 1 how we moved to Big Honkin' Goals by asking "Why?" Here's your chance to use it with someone else. Ask them about their goals, then ask, "Why is that important to you?" Listen carefully and you'll hear their values come right out. Pick a value you share and go for it!

THEM   It's a really cold day, isn't it? (Poor them. They must be suffering terribly to resort to discussing the weather.)

YOU   It sure is. I notice your name tag says you're from Dunder-Mifflin Paper. Are you a salesperson? (Asking about traits.)

THEM   I sure am. And you? (Poor them, still no clue.)

YOU   Nope. I'm a sanitation engineer. Why did you become a salesperson? (You just shifted to values.)

THEM   I really love interacting with people. (Aha! That's a value!)

YOU   Me, too! I really love it when I can connect with people, make new friends, and learn new things from them. What's your favorite part about people . . . ?

Voila! You're into a discussion based on values. Introverts like me will breathe a sigh of relief that we're discussing something "deep." Extraverts can simply be happy we're discussing at all. Everyone wins. Instead of wasting your time discussing mammatus clouds and whether they herald a coming apocalypse, you've wisely begun forging a bond that could last the rest of your life . . . or until the coming apocalypse, whichever comes first.

What's more intimate than values? Identity. When you can share with someone who you are and their sense of who *they* are, that brings real closeness. This is rarely a typical first conversation, but if you're doing great with values, why not go up to identity?

I have identity discussions by sharing who I am and simply letting the other person decide if they want to reciprocate at that level.

ME You know what's weird? I think of myself as an eternal nineteen-year-old, play-acting being a grownup business-person. I wonder if that ever changes?

THEM Er, excuse me. I think I have an incoming call. (They run as fast as humanly possible toward the nearest exit.)

Okay, that's a bit much for a first conversation, but identity-level conversation really brings you close to someone quickly.

When you're taking a conversation deeper, watch the other person. If they look uncomfortable with how deep you're going and/or how quickly, back off to a less-intimate level.

ME There I was, dressed as an elf, pondering its effects on my self-esteem . . . (noticing partner's look of consternation at this identity revelation) and I notice they have peel-and-eat shrimp here? Do you cook much? (back off to level of traits)

When your conversations become those in which you share more of who you are, you'll be able to deepen your bond with someone else. There's nothing wrong with simply telling stories about fun things that have happened to you, but those won't necessarily bring you closer. Sharing why those stories are important to you, and what they mean about you as a person . . . those revelations will forge a relationship.

GIVE TO STRENGTHEN A RELATIONSHIP

When you were just getting on someone's radar screen with your seven contacts, I suggested you help them with a problem, send them an article, et cetera. Now that you know what's important to them, you have an opportunity to give something you know they will find truly meaningful.

Giving turns out to be a quick and easy way to strengthen a relationship. It's much less work than begging them to like you, groveling on their doorstep, and going to therapy three times a week to find out why your relationships are so unsatisfying. Begging and therapy are the high-work way to strengthen a relationship. The low-work way is giving.

When I was a kid, grown-ups used to say, " 'Tis better to give than to receive." In what universe? Receiving treated me pretty well. In my world, Santa Claus brought me a train set. The Easter Bunny brought me chocolate eggs. And Lucrezia Demon of the Night brought me the tormented souls of my enemies. Giving wasn't high on my list.

So I was bummed when researchers showed that giving actually makes you happier than receiving. And the happiness lasts longer. Who knew? Thank you, researchers. The book *The Go-Giver* by Bob Burg and John David Mann even lays out the Law of Value: Always give more in value than you receive in payment. As a customer, we love getting more value than we paid for.

That's why JetBlue and Virgin America are so awesome—their coach class is better than other airlines' first class. It makes me want to fly them. A lot.

And . . . there's deeper psychology at work, too. Social psychologists call this principle "reciprocity." When someone does us a favor, we feel obliged to return it, many times over. They give us a free piece of chewing gum, we let them borrow our car and total it. If you doubt this principle, take a good look at your romantic relationships.

This makes sense! If we all give more than we receive, everyone wins. It bonds a community. Unless, of course, you're one of the 5 percent of the population who's sociopathic, and statistically, there are a lot of you reading this. In your case, you don't care about the community, but it still works for you: Reciprocity pretty much guarantees you'll get ahead by being generous.

You don't have to give *things*. Advice and assistance are giving. A friend asks a question via instant message, I call and solve her problem. It takes about thirty seconds. Giving accomplished! Then when I need her to come over and help me bake six dozen solstice cookies for the office party, she's there in a flash, cutting my work in half and entertaining me throughout with her creatively shaped cookie cutters.

People find handmade things or things that connect to their values especially meaningful. A handwritten thank-you card gets noticed. As does sending a parent an article about their kid's accomplishments with a handwritten congratulations. Or sending a Total Quality Freak the latest *Quality Control Pocket Reference* manual. And let's not even get started on people who are organization geeks and the potential to win their life favor with a simple trip to a fine stationery store!

In business, you can give more value than your payment in lots of ways. My philosophy is to give at least ten times the value I charge, and I charge a lot. That means my clients end up being people with very big goals. Otherwise, I can't deliver the high value-to-price ratio.

If you're in a service business, you can give in the form of extra service. Be available by e-mail or BlackBerry in ways that other people aren't. Deliver at unusual hours. Be a plumber who works noon to eight p.m. so you can charge daytime rates and provide service after people get home from work. Or wear a clown costume and make balloon animals for the kids while you fix the pipes. Be creative. You'll retain customers, generate word of mouth, and make it a lot less work to get more business.

You can give to anyone by just being nice. Smile. Compliment them. Bring them lunch when they're too busy to go out on their own. Help them when they didn't expect help. You'll be happier, and so will they. But you'll be even more happy, because it's better to give than to receive, remember?

At the end of the day, if we concentrate on giving, we'll be happier. People like hanging out with happy people, so our relationships will naturally deepen—even with the people we haven't been giving to. Since happy people get more done, faster, even when working alone, you'll get a double boost toward your goals.

END CONFLICT QUICKLY

No matter how close you become with someone, the time will come when you have a conflict. Conflict takes energy to sustain, time to resolve, and huge lawyers' fees that must be worked off. If you're pursuing the life of working less and doing more, the doing should *not* include conflict! That's just too much work. You're forming relationships so you can all have more of a life, not so you can spend your time fighting among yourselves.

Yet conflict does arise. Perhaps because you borrowed their flamethrower without asking. Or because they thought the trout mounted above your mantelpiece was still edible. These conflicts happen on two levels at once. The first is the substance of the conflict. Did someone borrow someone else's flamethrower or not? Does the fact they left the bones relatively intact on the mounting board make up for their impromptu dinner? I'll leave that to you to sort out. Here, we'll concentrate on the tricky part of conflict: the emotions. Conflict in *any* relationship calls into question the integrity of the relationship. If you both have strong personalities, what started as a little debate about grilling fish can turn into a knock-down-drag-out one around who's right and who's wrong, even if it really doesn't matter at this point.

I've found one of the most effective ways to defuse an argument quickly is to take the blame. Owning your own mistakes is considered admirable. Taking one for the team—even a team of two—is considered *divine*. Although you've worked through your blame, shame, and guilt issues, sadly, many others haven't. And when something goes wrong, rather than take responsibility, they'll look for anyone around to blame. That means you.

One man's boss told him to book a hotel in Las Vegas. He followed the instructions exactly, only to arrive and be treated to a boss temper tantrum. The boss had changed his mind. Bossyboy was wrong, but it was the employee who got blamed.

When you don't have the power, being right is irrelevant. Just like you and me, bosses like being right. When a boss has all the power, they'll win a right/wrong argument, every time.

In the grand scheme of things, most stuff in life isn't very important. A hotel reservation? Pretty trivial. For trivial things, just accept blame and fix things. Blamer-boy gets to feel like "The Decider," and you get to take the moral high road and feel superior.

When someone is irrationally angry because you followed their instructions, they'll interpret any defensiveness on your part as an attack. Instead, just say, "I'm very sorry, it's my fault, I must have misunderstood. What would you like me to do?" If you have a suggestion, say it now. The key is agreeing with your angry compatriot. Anger can't stand up to agreement. So take the blame, show remorse, and move into problem solving.

If the other person keeps blaming, just listen. It can be hard, but remember, they're not really mad at you. They're mad at their distorted, misremembered fantasy world. You just happen to be there. Nod. Agree quietly. Then ask, "What shall we do now?" Under no circumstances should you be defensive or snide or patronizing. That will just set them off again.

Sometimes, admitting guilt could have legal or career consequences. Let's say you're negotiating a big deal and your boss changes the deal terms at the last second. When the other party pulls out, boss-man gets furious and tries to blame you for it. Don't take the blame! In this case, it could hurt your career.

Do acknowledge the facts and acknowledge your boss's feelings. "Wow. The deal fell through. You're upset, I'm upset. What do you think we should do?" You are still acknowledging your boss's feelings, but you are carefully not admitting any fault that could open you up to liability or legal action.

You're still opting out of the "I'm right" game. You're acknowledging everyone's feelings, and then moving right along to book an even better suite at the Bellagio. (And that last bit of advice applies to your Las Vegas sales trip and your personal relationship!)

PREVENT CONFLICTS FROM ARISING IN THE FIRST PLACE

The quickest way to resolve conflicts is just not to have them in the first place. Rather than taking the blame, it's easiest to eliminate one of the most common ways relationships go sour: When they believe you've broken a promise. Learn to know when you're making promises, and make them with integrity.

Sometimes you'll make a promise that you just can't keep. You may say yes to something, truly believing you can deliver. But circumstances change. Tidal waves happen and you can't deliver on the original promise. Let people know sooner, rather than later. It can be uncomfortable saying, "It turns out, I can't deliver a barrel of monkeys. All I can deliver is a barrel of tuna fish, which won't have nearly the same surprise value." But if you say it sooner, people can find a backup plan and recover. Last-minute emergencies are an unpleasant surprise. They cast doubts on your reliability. The other person can ask, "If you weren't going to deliver, how come you didn't know until the last second?"

Even if you can confront changing circumstances, don't do this too often. Breaking agreements on a regular basis—even with good cause—gives you a bad reputation. Bad reputations chase away dependable people who help you work less, and attract dastardly bad guys who will hatch nefarious schemes then escape to far-away countries leaving you to clean up their mess. Keep your word and you'll attract good people.

I'm scared to admit when I'll miss a deadline. But people are often understanding. With notice, dates are flexible. You might say, "Gee, I had hoped that the monkeys would be here on Monday. It looks like I'm not going to be able to get them here." You might expect to get fired. Instead, they'll likely say, "Oh, okay. We can postpone the party until next Friday, giving us lots of time." Remember this when negotiating deadlines in the first place. There's no need to promise delivery tomorrow if you can promise it in two weeks. You can still deliver tomorrow, and be seen as underpromising and overdelivering (always a good thing), but that way, you have slack if you need it.

FIGHT FASTER WITH EXCUSE BOOKS

Relationships hit bumps. If you're going to have a conflict, do it fast! Have you noticed how much fights repeat? We have the same ones over and over and over. We even repeat the fights about fighting too much. If it repeats, it means we can create a system! (Oh, boy! I just *love* systems!)

Together, when you're calm and happy, create a word-processing document. Type in the excuses you each use over and over. My standard excuses include, "If only——hadn't happened, I would have been on time," "I don't have time to——," "It's not my responsibility to——," and "You don't——so I shouldn't have to——."

Group excuses into categories, so they're easy to find. One page has my "I'm Such a Victim" excuses, like, "Zombies ate my——" and "——isn't my fault!" Another page includes "Statements of the Obvious," with such genius as "But I was late" and "If only we had arrived on time, we wouldn't have missed——."

You each get a copy. Next time you start to argue, run (don't walk) to your nearest copy and hand it to the other person. Don't argue out loud. Instead, just tell your partner, "Statement of the Obvious, Excuse 3." Your partner can respond with a scathing "Self-fulfilling Prophecy Number 2." If either of you has a new line, say it and record the addition for next time. Voila! A two-hour argument now takes mere moments. You can look at each other, laugh a bit, and get back down to business.

Yes, this tip is serious. It works. It doesn't actually work because you're streamlining your arguments, it works because you're reminding yourselves how silly and futile arguing is in the first place. Life's too short. Excuse Books are for close relationships only! If you have strong, trusted relationships, you may be able to bring Excuse Books to work. But use your best judgment; they require mutual commitment to the relationship to work.

MAINTAIN YOUR EXISTING RELATIONSHIPS BY TAKING RESPONSIBILITY

Now that you've built strong relationships with people who will help you reach your goal of working less and doing more and now that you know how to maintain these relationships by resolving conflict quickly or avoiding conflict altogether, it's time to talk about how to maintain strong relationships with people you *have* to have relationships with—like coworkers. Maintaining good relationships with your coworkers will certainly help you work less and do more. When relations are strained, you spend your time picking needles out of your backside when someone "accidentally" leaves a cactus on your chair. When relations are good, you help them, they help you, the work gets done, and you can all go home early. Cacti never need become involved. (If you read the Introduction, you know the "go home early" is a total lie, but the rest really happens.)

Here's a shortcut to maintaining these relationships: Accept the blame for *everything*, and take full responsibility for the relationship. Doing so is what's called taking radical responsibility. You'll discover it's near magic how effortless your relationships will become. Never mind the emotional savings—mentally taking responsibility can be *quite* liberating—the time savings alone from abandoning "right vs. wrong" games is tremendous.

Consider blaming. When you accept the blame, you stop blaming others. They're happy to let you take the blame, and you can move on quickly. And blaming others doesn't actually help; it certainly doesn't cement relationships.

If you take full responsibility, you skip the blame and get right down to business. If your job requires paper, Billy's job is to order paper, and Billy never reorders. You can waste hours being upset, blaming Billy. It won't help; blocking your paper order is Billy's unconscious attempt to wrestle a tiny bit of power over an otherwise miserable life. So don't fight it. Save your time and effort and accept this as information. Billy isn't ordering paper. Asking hasn't worked. You can count on Billy to be late, but counting on Billy to suddenly start being prompt is silly and unrealistic.

Your best choice is to take full responsibility and find other solutions. Maybe you can help Billy set up automated reminders. Or maybe you can sit with Billy and help place the order. Or maybe you can redistribute responsibilities so Billy can do something where the deadlines don't matter so much.

"But I shouldn't have to sit down with Billy and place the order. That's not my job!" True. And remember, our goal is giving *you* an easy, work-less and do-more life. In terms of job responsibilities, Billy's failing and may get fired. Meanwhile, you need to do your job. It would be easier if you could count on Billy, but you can't. You can, however, take responsibility for the situation and do what it takes to help Billy succeed enough so *you* can get *your* job done faster.

What if this happens every day? "I shouldn't have to do Billy's job every day!" you cry. What's the alternative? Asking hasn't worked. Reminding hasn't worked. Now, it's decision time. The unordered paper is a given. What do you want to do about it? Lecturing won't work; you'll just waste more time and get more nothing done. So . . . you could help Billy approach your boss about getting proper training. You can help Billy learn to navigate the order system. Or you can decide that it's so bad that you talk to your boss about feeding Billy to your school of pet pirhanas. If your boss refuses, then you'll be ordering your own paper. You can accept it or fight it, but fighting will get you nowhere. The funny part is that when you fully take 100 percent responsibility, you feel free to make any of those choices, but without anger or resentment. If the situation is a real deal breaker, you can start circulating your résumé, on paper *you* bought, of course.

When you practice radical responsibility and the people around you are slackers, life goes from miserable to good, at least emotionally. But when you find others who also practice radical responsibility, it becomes sheer joy. That's because when each person takes full responsibility for everything getting done, you're all looking out for one another, offering help, and doing what it takes so the relationship itself is a success.

This is the purest expression of how relationships can help you work less and do more. With all of you providing a safety net for everyone else, you can all put your efforts into finding out how everyone can help everyone else succeed.

GIVE EFFECTIVE FEEDBACK TO GET BETTER RESULTS FROM YOUR RELATIONSHIPS

Okay, now we know how to build strong relationships and maintain good relationships with those people already in our life in order to work less and do more. But are we getting the best results we could from our relationships? Let's say you and your assistant, Terry, have bonded. Terry saves you gobs of time by making all your travel arrangements. But you notice that he always uses a travel agent who books you into your not-so-favorite hotel, the Rusty Bedpan. You call and change the reservation yourself because you don't want to confront Terry and tell him he didn't deliver. Rather than repeatedly correcting Terry's mistake yourself—which takes up your precious time—just correct the problem once, by providing feedback. This allows us one of our favorite things to do—tell people how much better their lives would be, if only they would listen to us.

"The way you booked that hotel was completely idiotic. I can't believe you didn't book through a Web site, you dolt. Let me show your feeble brain how it's done." Oddly, when we give our feedback, they don't appreciate it. They clearly haven't read the section in "Step 7: Optimize" on how feedback is a great source of learning and optimizing. It's up to us to take full responsibility, then, and give feedback in a way that they can hear it.

While you've no doubt mastered the art of hearing criticism, no matter how bluntly it's delivered, they haven't.° When you tell someone they're wrong, they'll immediately get defensive. Remember, in their mind, they're right and you're wrong; otherwise, they would already be doing things a different way. And yes, you think you're right about them being wrong, but maybe you're wrong about your being right.

Almost any feedback we're likely to give sends the message, "You're wrong." Using the famed "feedback sandwich," you give someone a compliment, then tell them they're wrong, then give them another compliment. Why would we do that? People know about the "feedback sandwich," so it doesn't work that well. People hear the compliment and just wait for the other shoe to drop. The compliment is seen as insincere, while the "you're wrong" message is thought of as "real."

Even if it does work, we lose. We've disguised our "you're wrong" message between two happy, "you're great" messages. Isn't this missing the point? The real message was "you're wrong"; "you're great" was just packing material. And now they're fixated on the packing material. That's not what we wanted.

Don't think about what you want them to fix. If you mention it, they'll hear you calling them wrong. Instead, think of what you want them to do in the future, instead of the wrong behavior. If they're letting the travel agent choose a hotel, what you want them to do is to book directly with a hotel or tell the agent

---

° You can always get them a copy of this book to help them learn to hear criticism. In fact, do yourself a favor: Buy a copy for everyone you know. In fact, you can even demonstrate the "Buy a spare" tip and buy two copies for each person. They'll love you twice as much.

which hotel to use. You won't say, "Don't let the travel agent choose a hotel." You will say, "Have the agent book me into the Golden Horseshoe or book me yourself."

I'll bet they love unasked-for advice as much as you do: Not at all.

Before you give advice, ask for permission. But again, don't say, "Would you like me to show you how to do that better?" That's just a thinly disguised version of, "you brain-dead moron. How could you do anything so foolish?" Instead, make an offer based on yourself and your experience: "I notice you're washing your pan upside down. I used to do that, too, and I discovered a trick that makes it work even better. Would you like me to share it?"

If they say no, then you get to work on your need to control them, since they're not open to your suggestion at the moment, and you can be sure unsolicited suggestions won't be listened to, either. If they say yes, then it's time to talk. Communications expert Shelle Rose Charvet offers a feedback format I really like.

You have permission and have phrased your suggestion as a future suggestion of what to do. Deliver the message. "I find it works better to hold the pan right side up when you wash it."

Next, give two reasons supporting your suggestion. Give one reason that tells them what the suggestion would accomplish, and give one reason that tells them what problem the suggestion would solve:

"If you book the hotel yourself or ask the agent to book a specific hotel, you'll save time booking the reservation and it will work better for all of us." (What the suggestion accomplishes.)

"Furthermore, if you specify the hotel, we won't have to worry about me arriving and having to deal with a new hotel, new facilities, and then getting all upset." (The problem the suggestion solves.)

Finish with something nice about the person or their abilities. "The rest of the reservations have been great. I really appreciate how much time and effort you put into making sure the travel plans are perfect."

Nowhere did we say or imply that what they were doing was wrong.

People are the ones who help you succeed, who get you access to the resources you need, and who generally can grease the wheels of life so your work is easier, faster, better, and stronger. But relationships themselves must be forged and maintained. You can forge them more strongly through repeated contact and increasing self-disclosure. You can maintain them by removing the ego conflict that comes from getting stuck in right/wrong games and instead keeping everyone moving toward your future goals. Many hands make light work, and when many hands are on your side, your work will be light, indeed.

CHAPTER RECAP

- Relationships are key to long-term success. Others help you succeed, help you get the resources you need, and can forge partnerships where each person does what's quick and easy for them.

- Get on someone's radar screen by having frequent, though not necessarily lengthy or deep, contact.

- Move from conversation about externalities and traits to values and identity to bond more closely.

- Give.

- Take the blame when things go wrong.

- Keep commitments, or raise the red flag early to preserve the relationship.

- Take 100 percent responsibility for the relationship, if preserving it is your goal.

- Give feedback emphasizing future action (punt the feedback sandwich).

STEP 9

LEVERAGE

The 9th and final step ties together everything we've done until now and boosts the effectiveness of every other step. Yes, it's leverage. Leverage is the Big Mama of working less and doing more. Big Mama takes no prisoners. You've heard of her. Leverage is common in business. Heck, I used to use it to sound smart. I would say things like, "We're going to leverage our abilities to create a world-changing product." (Yes, I was twenty-three once.) Then my mentor explained the definition of "leverage." He said when I used it incorrectly, I sounded like an overeager puppy dog—young, clueless, and slightly slobbery in a really cute way.

The word *leverage* comes from the physics of simple machines, specifically, the lever (quelle surprise). "Leverage" in the business world means getting outsized results without having to put in more resources or work. Taking a coworker to lunch day after day, hoping enough seafood salad will convince them to help write a report is a big use of time and effort. Tickling their feet with an ostrich feather until they agree to help takes about forty-five seconds; it's a very high-leverage activity.

When everything in life is humming like a well-oiled machine, finding greater leverage will boost your results without more work. You'll almost certainly *change* what you get done, but the point of leverage is that you needn't do more work.

There's no magic formula for finding leverage. This is where your creativity comes into play. Your creativity plus this final chapter, that is. You're in the home stretch, where we'll learn to take *any* technique for working less and doing more and turbocharge it to get even bigger results. We'll be exploring several different strategies you can use to create leverage in your life.

AUTOMATE TO GET LEVERAGE

Once, most of the human race spent much of their time picking cotton, spinning thread, weaving fabric, sewing clothes, and looking flashy to land the mate of their dreams. Automation changed all that. We built the systems to do the work for us: the cotton gin, automated looms, sewing machines, and Match.com. Now, we spend our lives doing little of that. The machines do it for us.

Automation is a powerful form of leverage. You spend a small amount of time up front to automate a task, and you save tons and tons and tons of time as the automation frees you from doing the task. You probably have neither the time nor the metalworking skill to build a factory to automate your life; fortunately, though, we rarely do anything real these days. We just manipulate information, and for that, we have mankind's most awesome device ever, the computer.

In our "Step 3: Conquer Technology," we saw that technology can be a big time suck. But there's another side to the story. When you use technology thoughtfully, to automate things that take a lot of time, you get tremendous leverage. An hour spent automating a task with your computer can save you hours or days going forward.

Automate Your Research

One task that you can automate is research. Many information sites will let you save your searches so you can easily perform them at a moment's notice. Use this capability! Rather than remembering you needed the entire phrase "care and feeding of white cats rescued from evil supergenius" to get a list of specialty pet care stores, just bookmark the search. Next time your boss's cute little vixen starts coughing up too many hairballs, your search will be waiting for you so you can get back to your actual work responsibilities. My favorite way to automate research is Google Alerts, a service that will send you a daily notice of any new articles that match the search you've created. It's pure leverage: Set up the search once for the name of your employer, and never think of it again. And you'll *still* be alerted first to read the details of the suit filed against your company by your coworkers who claim they thought "we'll handcuff you to your desk until you finish your project" was just a figure of speech. No need to spend time daily doing research; only when there's a real result or new development will you ever need to think about it.

Any job that involves keeping tabs on what's happening in the world can use automated research. If you're tracking your competitors to figure out their secret plans or if you're keeping up on new developments in your field, automated alerts are for you. If you're in sales or have important relationships with customers, vendors, or partner companies, you can set up alerts to tell you when something newsworthy happens. You'll be first on the phone after the news hits with appropriate praise or condolences. "I'm *so* sorry about that chemical explosion. I'm always here if you need to talk. Meanwhile, would you mind settling up your account before your assets get frozen by the court?"

Automate Your Reminders

One place automation works wonders is with tickler files. A tickler file is a reminder system, different from the coworker Ostrich Feather Persuasion technique presented earlier. When you know your license to own Zombie Reanimation Powder expires next March, you file the renewal papers in your tickler file under *March*. Since you check the file every day, when the time comes, the paper reminds you that it's time to renew. Since you filed the application in the file, even the paperwork is right there.

That's still too much work for me. Check a tickler file every *day*? Not likely. It might interfere with sleeping late. So my reminders are automated. The only work is setting up the reminder. There's no daily checking—when the reminder is needed, it magically arrives. I use deferred e-mail for reminders. With deferred e-mail, an e-mail of my choice gets magically sent to me sometime in the future. It's a reminder system I can trust, since I check e-mail daily and am not likely to stop. E-mails can be scheduled as far in advance as ten years. In 2018—assuming we survive the 2012 Mayan Armageddon—I'm due for a tetanus shot booster. On the upcoming front, the confirmation e-mails and relevant documents for a conference I'm attending will be arriving in December, a few days before the conference. All the work I used to do collecting paperwork, filing it, and then hoping to remember it when I needed it . . . gone! Everything becomes an e-mail attachment that magically arrives at the appointed time.

Since services come and go, rather than putting recommendations right here in the book, I've listed deferred e-mail services on this book's resource Web site, GetItDoneGuyBook.com.

Automate Your Purchases

And of course the computer is great for automating regular commerce. You can use technology to set up regular salary payments for your henchmen so they don't revolt (they're already revolting enough). If you often order the same stationery supplies, you can create "favorites" lists so a single click will place your favorite order. Technology even makes ordering take-out a snap—most cities have online services that deliver meals from participating restaurants right to your door. This is huge for those of us who have phobias of turning on a stove or actually cooking from scratch. My regular weekly, monthly, quarterly, and yearly orders are just a click away.

Some things don't get reordered at a regular time, but rather when they run out, like checks, toner cartridges, or replacement nose hair clipper blades. You can write the reorder reminder on a sticky note and tape it to the last item. When you go to use the last one you have, the sticky note is your reminder it's time to reorder. I might even include the order form or reorder URL in an attached envelope. I'm putting in a small effort to set up the reminder and saving potentially huge time and hassle of running out of something right when I need it most. (For you total quality geeks in the audience, this is your own personal version of kanban.)

USE SIGNS TO LEVERAGE

Not everything has to be done with high technology, however. Pencil and paper is such a powerful source of leverage that it revolutionized the world. It's everywhere, now, so we don't even remember how great it is. I sleep with a pencil and paper under my pillow, just to be close to such amazingness. Pencil and paper automate information transmission. Think "signs." You can automate information—put signs—in all kinds of places. Instead of telling each visitor that the coat closet is to the right of the reception area, put up a sign. Rather than explaining to each person interrupting you that you're in focus mode, make a sign. Use minisigns (we call them "labels") for your supply closet so you know where everything is. Write up instructions on how to get to your office or house from the airport, bus terminal, and via highway. When guests are due, just toss them the instruction sheet. The leverage is immense! A single investment in creating a sign pays for itself over and over in eliminating the need for explanations, research, and memory.

The long-term savings makes it well worth the time to create the sign in the first place. If you need the sign for an event that happens over and over, like the annual shareholders' meeting or a Cub Scout convention, file the signs with your notes on the event. Each time you put on the event, just grab the signs and reuse them. I have a single word-processing document with all the signs needed to have a fabulous party at my apartment. One touch of the Print icon and setup is a snap: "Please put your coats downstairs," "Talk quietly on the deck after 1 a.m. so you don't disturb the neighbors," and "Don't eat these, they're made of plastic."

REUSE TO LEVERAGE YOUR TIME, MONEY, AND RESOURCES

In addition to automating, the second powerful form of leverage comes from reusing stuff. For me, this lesson came from socks. I used to buy cheap socks to save money. Then I discovered if you actually wash your socks and wear them again, your clothing bill goes way, way down. Taking it a step further, if you buy more expensive socks that are made out of cloth instead of paper, they can look good for *years*. This works for all clothes, not just socks. And it works for your work life, too, not just your fashion choices.

By reusing something, you leverage the time, effort, or money it took to create whatever you're reusing by saving on the need to replace or dispose of it. This seems obvious, sure, but think deeply about it.

It's way expensive to get new customers. So why not leverage your existing customers by reusing them, and saving yourself the time and expense of getting new ones? Reuse them by selling them new products, or by renting your product instead of selling it. When they rent, they just send you tons of money every month. Xerox's first copier machines were rented, not purchased. By reusing their customers month over month, Xerox executives were actually able to *bathe* in money—all through the miracle of leveraging their customer base to save the effort of getting new customers.

If you're in a job where you write or create content, leverage your writing by reusing it. You can design a speech and use the text of the speech as an article. You can post the article on your blog as a blog post, and then post a video of you reading the article as a video blog. You create the content once and use it for lots of different purposes. If you printed drafts of the article on paper, you can even use that paper as hand towels when you forget to reorder paper towels (you didn't automate your reorder system, did you?).

IDENTIFY YOUR CURRENCIES TO LEVERAGE

More leverage comes from the fact that you have a ton of valuable stuff, only you don't realize it's valuable. You have skills, things, and access that are valuable to others that you take for granted, if you bother to notice them at all. Other people have skills, things, and access that *they* take for granted, that you might value. We'll call these hidden gems "currencies." You can find leverage by trading currencies that are cheap for you but valuable to others for things that are cheap for others, but valuable for you. You both win. Rather than spending your time and effort building what you value from scratch, a simple swap gives you both great benefit without doing the work yourself.

Currencies come in all shapes and sizes. Professor Neck owns a copy of a rare book on Egyptian mummification techniques used to preserve pets for the afterlife. She's read it a dozen times, committed it to memory, and though it sits on her shelf, she will probably never read it again. She's finishing her latest book, and the constant interruptions of academic life are driving her crazy. She needs somewhere quiet and relaxing where she can focus completely, contemplating anything but mummies.

Her friend Sebastian owns a time-share condo in Aruba that he bought when taking a "free" trip that he won in a sweepstakes. Sebastian isn't thinking about Aruba, though. His pet dachshund is suffering with a deadly illness and he's completely distraught. He's been frantically searching for a way to keep his dachshund with him for eternity.

Use Your Things as Currencies

Can you spot how these two can leverage their currencies? By exchanging her book for use of her friend's condo, Professor Neck can escape the interruptions, focus, and finish her book. Sebastian can stop wasting his time consulting oracles and raising demons by leveraging the time-share. It's essentially free for him, and with Professor Neck's book, he's got the key to eternal afterlife for his dachshund. Or failing that, a *really* lifelike centerpiece for his dining room. Everyone wins!

Buildings and space are common thing-currencies. Wainwright Bank in Massachusetts realized they weren't using their office space after hours. Local nonprofits needed meeting space.

Wainwright Bank was looking for ways to expand its brand to new customers. Without spending time coming up with new sales pitches or marketing plans, Wainwright easily became a bank of choice by trading after-hours access to their Community Rooms for the nonprofits' banking business. The nonprofits needed bank accounts anyway, and they traded their customership in return for Wainwright office space. The nonprofit didn't need to waste valuable resources searching out office space and could instead devote their energies to raising money—their main goal. Neither side did an ounce of extra work or spent any extra money, they just traded currencies that were valuable to each other.

An extreme example of thing-based leverage is a celebrity autograph. It's virtually free for a celebrity to create an autograph, and some autographs can be sold for gazillions of dollars, saving said celebrity the backbreaking work of having to show up on time and perform for their money. If you have nothing else you can leverage as a currency, simply become a world-famous celebrity and then use your autograph as currency. It's simple as pie.

You might not have things that others value, but you may have access. Perhaps your friendship with eighth-grade-nerd-turned-hipster-doorman Melvin Goldblatt helps you get into the hottest club in town while others wait for hours. That currency can be terribly valuable when your client confides that they've always wanted to see the famed velvet wallpaper inside. You can get them in, earn their undying devotion (does undying devotion mean vampires? I just *love* vampires!), and just as importantly, their undying business—with far less work than giving them a dozen pseudo-persuasive computer presentations with sparkly text.

In addition to hipness, you might have access to information, education, trade shows, or other events. Many corporate trainers staff events with students and people who could never afford to pay for training. It costs nothing but a chair to add an extra person, and the trainers leverage that into several days' worth of free or low-cost assistance because that same chair is quite valuable to others. Rather than working to earn the money to pay assistants, they trade currencies, and everybody gets what they need.

Access to people is valuable when you can be in a matchmaker position, poised to introduce two who want to meet each other. This happens all the time in business, when people are looking for clients, suppliers, mentors, and employees. You save them both the effort of finding each other, and you're giving *both of them* the gift of each other in one quick introduction. Since giving is a cornerstone of relationships, you deepen *two* relationships with a single introduction.

One of the most powerful things you can reuse is your strengths and skills. We're usually taught to focus on our weaknesses so we end up average at everything. *Yawn!* That means *everything* will be work. But if we know what comes so easily to us that it's like breathing (for example, breathing), it's obvious that a great way to work less and do more is by finding ways to reuse those skills whenever you can, while weaseling out of work that can't be done with your strengths.

All those years spent stuck in front of your computer may have given you an unusually deep grasp of computers. Maybe something about the way you deal with people makes groups you're in work really well together. Or you could be great at finding just the right words to express a concept, or maybe you can be funny in just the right way to help people confront difficult situations with humor.

Skills are essentially free for you to use. You've spent the time and effort to get good at them, and now you can leverage them by doing what's easy for you but unusually valuable for others. My coaching career got started this way. I was working at a normal day job and one day went to lunch with an executive friend of mine. We spent the lunch discussing a problem of his. At the end of lunch, he said, "These talks are so valuable! Do you realize I would gladly pay you large sums of money for these conversations?" I thought fast, saying, "Do you realize I would gladly *bill you* large sums of money for that conversation?" I sent a bill. He paid it. And I discovered that my skill at asking questions and cutting to the heart of a matter was easy for me, yet very, very valuable for others. It was a great opportunity for leverage. I took a skill that was effortless for me but valuable to others and created a lucrative business. When you can use your effortless skills to make money, you work just a fraction of the time to get the same results that would take forever using non-strengths.

The strengths that will give you the most leverage are the ones that come to you as naturally as breathing. The good news is that you have them. The bad news is that, like breathing, they're so natural you never notice them. On some occasions, I have asked friends, clients, and colleagues to tell me what value they think I bring to my friends, life, and work. They help pinpoint the personality traits that years of business brainwashed me into believing were worthless: my sense of humor, creativity, inspiration, and my obsessive compulsive need to organize everything in sight. And what's a good way to leverage those traits? Oh, I don't know . . . maybe a podcast and a book where I invite people to share my .38 mm roller-ball pen fetish with humor and creativity. The book's resource site has links to online tools you can use to survey your friends and find the currencies you can use for leverage.

Your other source of currencies is to review the wealth inventory you created in "Step 2: Stop Procrastinating." Not only does that list wealth for your own use, but every item in your inventory can become a building block you can leverage by finding people and situations where that item is more valuable to others than it is to you.

FIND LEVERAGE BY COMBINING

Ever since I learned that $1 + 1 = 3$, my favorite source of leverage is combining. Combining lets you work toward one goal, and get progress for free toward other goals.

One masterpiece of combining comes from Caroline, the CEO of a software company. Instead of using separate systems for e-mail and her task list, she leverages her e-mail time by combining her e-mail handling, to-do tracking, and reminders. She e-mails to-do items to her e-mail. Her inbox is her to-do list. For incoming e-mail that doesn't require immediate action, she deletes it or uses deferred e-mail to have the e-mail and relevant attachments sent back to her inbox when she thinks she'll be ready for it. She gets the goodness of both e-mail and task lists, without needing separate programs. By using e-mail for everything, she doesn't need to learn to use, upgrade, back up, and synchronize a task list program for her to-dos. She just e-mails herself a note, it becomes a to-do, and she starts getting things done.

When she gets into work, her inbox is the center of her workspace. It becomes a tool for moving forward, even as new e-mail comes in. For me, with separate systems, e-mail is a huge distraction, because when I'm looking at my e-mail, my task list—which is what kicks me into *useful* action—is far away. Caroline's combined system saves the effort of maintaining two systems, and it keeps her action triggers front and center at all times.

While Caroline combines tools, you can combine tasks to make progress on two fronts while doing just one task. If you're summarizing a team project for a report or paper, you can even leverage your normal team conversation by combining requests for clarification with creating the summary. E-mail your work group saying, "Do I understand the problem correctly? Here are my thoughts." Then write the executive summary then and there. Writing to specific people will help you stay conversational and crystallize your thoughts around the needs of that audience. And since e-mail is two-way, their response will help you understand what you need to clarify for the final paper. Best of all, they never need to know they're helping you write the paper that will get you promoted to become their boss. They do the work of double-checking your summary, and you end up with a great, accurate summary without needing to do the work to check it yourself.

There's no magic formula in finding ways to combine tasks. You can train yourself to find opportunities by choosing a task or goal you have to complete. Think through how you'll do it. Then choose another task at random, and ask, "What can I do to make progress on *both* these tasks at once?" Christine Hohlboum, author of the most excellent book *The Power of Slow*, needed a break from her work doing public relations for a musician client. She decided to grab a movie and give herself a "me-day." By the end of the movie, she realized she could also help her client by watching the credits of the locally produced film for the names of local organizations that might need a composer. Instead of a separate research effort, she simply found a way her leisure time could help her work toward goals.

A student leader in a college government wanted to learn how to gain respect among the different groups he worked with, students, faculty, and other students. Since he had virtually *no* free time, he asked, "How can I learn about building respect in the course of my normal duties?" He realized he often met with the very people whose respect he wanted to gain. Rather than making small talk about the weather, he decided to make small talk by asking them, "What are the qualities of the kind of people you like to work with?" A tiny change in his small talk could produce a vast difference in his development as a leader. Doing the same amount of work, he's now doing his job, learning to build respect, and actually *building it* at the same time—which is clearly *doing* a lot more.

You can even leverage what you do in your free time by combining your leisure Web surfing with doing real work. Since we all love reading blogs and posting obnoxious responses, it would be great to use that to move our goals forward and get our work done at the same time. And it's possible! You can use blog posts to spur on writing entire speeches, white papers, or reports. If you're writing on a certain topic, say, ad copy extolling the joys of comfy chairs, find some horrid blogger who takes an opposite point of view. Perhaps a Pilates trainer or someone who advocates running daily. Browse their blog until you find a particularly heinous post that gets your blood boiling, and then respond. But respond intelligently, coherently, and using complete sentences. In fact, use the emotional energy to drive you, and trigger writing your masterpiece.

"I admire your stance on jogging. Jogging in urban areas on concrete has been shown to cause lower back damage if done without proper equipment. To recover, people must spend time in comfy chairs. Why not skip the injury and go straight to the comfy chair?" A simple cut and paste and you have your ad copy.

You don't even need to post your blog comment. In fact, check the blog's copyright. If you're giving up rights to your masterpiece by posting it, just use the blog for emotional inspiration and then cut and paste the blog post into a word processing document. You're writing an ad and amusing yourself on the Web with a single, simple activity. You've had fun playing *and* saved the hours it would have taken you to write the copy at your desk.

LEVERAGE YOUR ADDRESS BOOK

Your address book also provides the chance for combining tasks, saving work, and getting work done quickly. For years, I tracked prospects in a fancy "customer relationship management" (CRM) system. I felt *so* sophisticated, dutifully spending time and money synchronizing my desktop, the Web, and my handheld, entering my times of last contact, my prospect's favorite wines, details about where in the sales cycle they were, and . . . yada yada yada.

Then I realized my CRM system could be combined with my address book by using the address book notes field to do everything the sophisticated CRM system did. The secret was realizing that a notes field can hold more than just notes.

The address book notes field could track our contact history, juicy gossip, and the payment schedule for "discretion" payments they send so we don't reveal the juicy gossip. And the CRM sales process tracking could turn into keywords in the notes field. I put a "_" before each keyword, so they wouldn't get confused with words that might appear in the text note. _PROSPECT goes in the notes field for any new prospect. When they hire me, I change it to _CLIENT. If they decide not to hire me, I can change it to _MISGUIDED SOUL.

You can create "smart folders" or searches that will select everyone with a given keyword in their notes field. You can use business keywords like _PROSPECT, _CLIENT, _VENDOR. You can use social keywords like _DinnerPartyInvite and _PartyAnimal. Since the keywords are just address book notes, they synchronize across all my machines and my handheld devices, without the need to recreate distribution lists everywhere. By using my Address Book Notes field for notes about each prospect *and* keywords, I no longer need separate tools and distribution lists to manage all the ways I might want to contact someone.

LEVERAGE YOUR BIG NUMBERS

The last form of leverage gets you larger results through the power of big numbers. Small things can be multiplied for huge results by spreading them widely. A creator of educational programs spent two years developing a network of thirty thousand affiliate distributors. That was a lot of work for two years. But now, the moment he releases a product, almost every affiliate buys one to keep in stock. He's leveraged his two years of network building into thirty thousand sales for *every product he creates*. It's a fabulous example of leveraging large numbers.

Spending time creating broad distribution and audience can often leverage a single product into building a bigger business. A recent college grad started a commerce Web site. He told me he was tempted to develop new products, but found that new products didn't move the business forward nearly as much as finding new marketing outlets. He got more business results in the same amount of time by expanding the number of people he reached, not by expanding the number of products he offered. He created just enough product to keep his existing customers coming back, and spent most of his time marketing and expanding his reach.

One of the most powerful uses of large numbers in your daily life is building a reputation (or in twenty-first-century parlance, a personal brand) out in the world. Having a lot of people who know and respect you can make it much easier to find jobs, do research quicker, and call on others for career help, which can save you a lot of time. We covered a lot of the specifics needed for building strong relationships in step 8.

Once you have that strong network built, you can leverage the heck out of it. If you need help finding a job, if you have a strong community of five hundred people, sending out one single request for help could produce five leads, even if only 1 percent of your community is able to help. That sure beats what one of my friends did—sending out 250 résumés to companies, hoping for a callback. You can also tap your community for help solving problems; people are often willing and happy to help people with whom they feel a genuine connection. Even if you're not sure what help you need, asking your network for help framing the problem can bring you great insight. You build the network once and get its benefits for life. And its benefits all boil down to asking a large number of people for a small favor. What comes back can be huge.

Leverage is the art of putting in very little effort and getting oversized results. In the "work-less, do-more" world, the more you can find leverage in everything you do, the more life will become an extended vacation with an occasional, refreshing foray into work.

CHAPTER RECAP

- Leverage gets outsized results from modest effort.

- Automate to get leverage; automate research, reminders, and purchases.

- Reuse what you produce to leverage the effort of creation in multiple ways.

- Get leverage from your currencies, gaining leverage by finding people who value your currencies.

- Find leverage by combining (but not multitasking!) tasks.

- Leverage large numbers. Build a broad distribution channel, and/or a strong network, and a single small effort can produce results that multiply across your entire network.

THE END . . . OR, RATHER, THE BEGINNING

Thank you for joining me on this journey of working less and doing more. We've covered a lot, from procrastination to filing to relationships to leverage. Even though we've done nine steps and gone over tons of tips, everything really boils down to knowing why you're here, orienting your life around that, and not sweating the small stuff when you wander off your path. And make no mistake, we all wander off the path. The trick is noticing when we do and getting back on track.

Now it's almost time to close the book, get up from your chair, and walk out into your life. Before you do, spend a moment to consider why you picked up this book in the first place, and what you can do today to make that come true. Perhaps you'll complete something at work faster so you can actually take a lunch break. Or maybe you'll find a better way to reach a current goal. Just one final tip: Zombies don't follow orders very well, so if you're determined to take over the world, robots could be a superior choice.

Please, go forth and *do* take over the world. Do it by helping everyone around you work a little less and live a little more. If we all conspire to be a little smarter, stronger, and faster, we can go home early. And home is where our life is. It's where our shmoopie is. And our kids. And our cat Fluffy, and Bernice's boa constrictor. And . . . wait a minute. Has anyone seen Fluffy since Bernice dropped off her boa? Fluffy? *Fluffy??* I have to go.

Come visit me on the Web at www.SteverRobbins.com, share your stories about working less and doing more, and enjoy the Get-It-Done Guy podcast. Until we meet again, I remain most humbly yours, Stever Robbins, the Get-It-Done Guy.

ACKNOWLEDGMENTS

Writing acknowledgments is fun and scary. Fun because I get to thank lots of wonderful people. Scary because I might forget someone and then be mightily embarrassed when they confront me publicly during the book tour, wrestle me into submission, assume my identity, and go on to become a national celebrity.

The ones who made everything possible were Grammar Girl Mignon Fogarty, Richard Rhorer, Grigory Tovbis, and Emily Rothschild at Macmillan. They took a chance on me to host the Get-It-Done Guy, and then to write a book. (Emily, how do you manage to make me feel great, as you ask me to rewrite a chapter for the third time?)

Jeff Quinlan, my partner and teammate, did everything in his power to help me finish, encouraging me relentlessly throughout the entire process. He helped me stay on track even during the rough patches, when I came close to renouncing modern civilization and joining a Buddhist monastery (writing a book is *not* easy). He kept me as healthy and happy as possible.

Tamin Pechet regularly called to explore productivity, my purpose in writing the book, and different structures and themes. He gave more excellent ideas than I can count. He stuck with me from start to finish, and was the best brainstorming partner ever.

Case Prince provided his apartment, computer with amazing 2560x1600 monitor, and pet cat Lulu for six solid weeks of writing and tummy rubs (for Lulu, who was not to be denied).

Lord Aaron Shimoff of Middlesex kicked off the book with a daylong writing session in his apartmentlike palace. Then he abandoned me to get an MBA at Babson, where he invited me for a tour. I ended up working there. Aaron is an amazing catalyst for many things.

Marion Kahn shaped the very first outline and turned my transcribed babblings into prose. My former-and-future publicist Amy Logan read the whole thing on a day's notice when I needed to do major restructuring. Agent Lisa Queen also contributed at several points in the writing process.

Joel Kehle listened when I needed to talk and talked when I needed to listen, as he has since sophomore year in college. Jay Laird set me up for many small smiles, instead of one big one; small successes kept me going! Michael Neill, my friend and former coach, put me on the path of following my passion, which led to the Get-It-Done Guy podcast and this book. Tyler Duckworth, trainer and entertainment industry gossip source, whipped my body into shape despite my whining and complaining so I could start each day with vim, verve, and vigor.

The Get-It-Done Guy Community. I am humbled by how many people have become part of my extended Get-It-Done Guy community. My last month of writing was a month of Action Days. Regular attendees became my writing community: Welton Hong, Sarah McQueen, Breset Walker, Jessica Hammerman, Collin, Sam Rogers, Laurie, and Jen Waller. All the Action Day attendees shared their own successes and kept each other going: Sharon M., Shaina Hammerman, Heather, Patti, Russell, Debra, Jeff Layton, Mike, Wayne, Rosemary, Karen, Wayne Buckhanan, Amanda Trombley, Tracy, Michelle Muto, Beth, Sheila, Jeff Lehtinen, Mia Taylor, Amy Hamilton, Thida, Michael Purpura, Bernette, Matt Deaton, Nan Pitcher, Heather Wilaby, Rachel, Luis Huegel, Rosy Escandon, Denise Bike, Nikki Van Dusen, Marlena Corcoran, Kirsten Dixson, Elizabeth, Blaine, That Brad Guy, Lionel Wilson, Katie, Peter, Michael Steffens, Jim Woodell, Paula, Michael Kindness, Lee, Kathie, Pam Teagarden, Robert, Keith Murray, Forrest Wright, Steven Harper, Bob, Doug, David, Alex Zarazua, Yasmeen, Amy, Wayne Twitchell, Jack Wooten, Jessica, Mike, Tricia, Nancy, Tina Abate, Richie, Ryan, Roland, Yasmine Ba, Vince Lyons, Robert, Michelle Trombley, Sarah, Sielke, Paula, Steve, Scott, Sherri Austin, Shoshana, Rebecca, Susan, Susan Prestage, Raz, Sarah, Steve, Michelle Mjuto, Christina, Ebony Caldwell, Freya, Gary, Christine Cohn, Dan, Dwight, Heidi Miller, Iza, Heath Rassner, Heather, Aaron, Amy, Andrew, Angela, Ainsley, Alejandra, Alicia McLucas, Cheryl, Chris, Chris Christensen, Annabelle, Beth, Carmen, Kimberlee Oakes, Lisa Hamaker, Malia Kawaguchi, Mario Phillipides, Laura, Lee, Melanie, Mica, Michael, Marky-Warren, Mary-Kim, Max, Jackie, Jennifer, Jennifer Ammirati Doyle, James Connors, Jasmine, Jason, Jordan Atlas, Kate, Katherine, John B. Corey Jr., Jon-Terryia.

And last but not least, a big thank-you to my Twitter and Facebook followers who helped me explore ideas through my blog. Tara, Tania Arpa, Cara, Bruce Byrne, Greg, Dan Weiss, Laurent Duperval, Luis H, Gary H, Bob, Jim Sewell, Tom Flesher, Carol Skolnick, Rich G, Karoline Gostl, Alec, Rodrigo, Vince Lyons, Vin Addala, Nate Winn, Rob Hooft, Carl Dierschow, Nancy, Kate, MJ, Jeff, Lenore, AJ, Laurie, Chip Cullen, Tyler Lars Groll, Stefania, Jeremie, Alexander M, Rachel B, Kelly, Bob Kerns, Scott Cunningham, Peakaytay, Craig C, JT, Jaclyn, Leanne, Bonnie Taylor, Ryan, Wayne Buckhanan, Bill, Steve, Erin Lancione, Robert Wallace, Mark MacLeo, and Gregg Sanderson. Who also happens to be my father.

Thanks!

INDEX

ABOUT THE AUTHOR

STEVER ROBBINS created the Quick and Dirty Tips network's Get-It-Done Guy podcast. An executive coach, professional speaker, and member of nine startups, he cofounded FTP Software and managed the creation of the Quicken VISA Card. He is also an adjunct lecturer at Babson College, where he lectures on entrepreneurship-related topics. Stever holds a Bachelor's from MIT and an MBA from Harvard. He lives in Cambridge, Massachusetts.

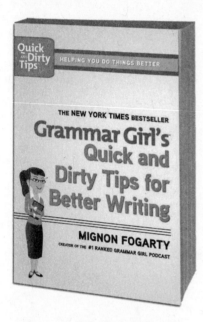